Creole Compositions & Stories from Louisiana

A Collaborative Musical Ethnography
by Bruce Sunpie Barnes and Rachel Breunlin

with

Original Songs and Arrangements
by Bruce Sunpie Barnes and Leroy Joseph Etienne

Essays
by Rachel Breunlin

Translations
by Bruce Sunpie Barnes, Leroy Joseph Etienne,
and Rachel Breunlin

Artwork
by Francis X. Pavy

L'Union Creole
&
The Neighborhood Story Project
with
The University of New Orleans Press

© 2019
All Rights Reserved

Library of Congress Cataloging-in-Publication Data

Names: Barnes, Bruce Sunpie, 1963- author. | Breunlin, Rachel, author. | Etienne, Leroy, author.
Title: Le Ker Creole : Creole Compositions and Stories from Louisiana /
by Bruce Sunpie Barnes, Rachel Breunlin & Leroy Etienne.
Description: New Orleans : University of New Orleans Press, 2019.
Identifiers: LCCN 2018057617 | ISBN 9781608011728 (hardcover, cd)
Subjects: LCSH: Creoles--Louisiana--Music--History and criticism. | Folk music--Louisiana--History and criticism.
Popularmusic--Louisiana--History and criticism. | Ethnology--Louisiana. | Creole dialects--Louisiana.
Classification: LCC ML3560.C25 B37 2019 | DDC 781.62/410763--dc23
LC record available at https://lccn.loc.gov/2018057517

Series Editor: Helen A. Regis
Graphic Designer: Gareth Breunlin
Photo Editor: Bruce Sunpie Barnes
Cover Art by Francis X. Pavy

Music produced by Bruce Sunpie Barnes, Leroy Joseph Etienne, Matt Hampsey, and Michael Harris.
Original songs by Bruce Sunpie Barnes and Leroy Etienne.
Recorded in Louisiana with Ben Mumphrey and Jay Wesley at Studio in the Country;
Tony Daigle and Steve Nails at Dockside Studios;
Danny Kadar, Joe Stolarik, and Charles Butler at the New Orleans Jazz Museum at the Old U.S. Mint;
and Justin Armstrong at the Neighborhood Story Project.
Mixed by Mark Bingham at Piety Street Studios and Tony Daigle at Dockside Studios.
Mastered by Paul Orofino.

Band
Bruce Sunpie Barnes (*Vocals, Accordion, and Harmonica*)
Matthew Hampsey (*Guitar and Banjo*)
Michael Harris (*Bass and Background Vocals*)
Leroy Joseph Etienne (*Vocals and Drums*)

Special Guests
Detroit Brooks (*Guitar*), Donald "Dut" Claude (*Tambourine and Vocals*),
Clarence Delcour (*Tambourine and Vocals*), Molly Ducoste (*Violin*),
Rex Gregory (*Tenor Saxophone*), Erica Falls (*Vocals*), Louis Ford (*Clarinet and Tenor Saxophone*),
Fred Johnson (*Tambourine and Vocals*), Joe Lastie (*Drums*), Kerry Lewis (*Upright Bass*),
Eric Lucero (*Trumpet*), Ricky Monie (*Piano*), and the Panorama Brass Band.

The Neighborhood Story Project
P.O. Box 19742
New Orleans, LA 70179
www.neighborhoodstoryproject.org

Le Kèr Creole was made possible by generous support from
the New Orleans Jazz National Historical Park,
the University of New Orleans, the Surdna Foundation,
Preservation Hall, and the New Orleans Jazz Museum at the Old U.S. Mint.

In Memory of

Will Ainsworth

Fernest Arceneaux

Indiana Norris Barnes

Willie Barnes, Sr.

Bernadette

Clarence "Jockey" Etienne

Lawrence Etienne

Odelia Porter Etienne

Cecile Etienne Girouard

Michael Hampsey

Jim Kebodeaux

Bobby Matthews

Jonathan Scott

Lucille Etienne Thomas

&

Daniel "Ice Cube Slim" Untermyer

Francis X. Pavy's "Guardian Two." Augmented photographic lithophane in carved acrylic. Image courtesy of Arthur Roger Gallery.

Mèrsi | Thank You

To New Orleans Jazz National Historical Park for being the first national park in the country dedicated to music, and for sharing the cultures of the region that have produced songs beloved around the world. To Matt Hampsey, supervising interpretive park ranger, for continuing the partnership between the park and the Neighborhood Story Project (NSP), pulling us all together for this collaboration, co-producing the music, and playing guitar and banjo on the songs. To Joseph Llewellyn, former superintendent of the New Orleans Jazz National Historical Park, who loves this music and was an advocate in helping us develop the infrastructure to work together. And to Lance Hatten, former superintendent of Jean Lafitte National Historical Park, for supporting the project along the way. To Karen Armangost for believing in the power of ethnography as a tool of interpretation, and to Bud Holmes and Richard Johnson, wonderful stewards of our shared books and programs, for working with us on curriculum. And to Nick Spitzer, whose report to Jean Lafitte is one of the foundations of Afro-Creole studies in Louisiana.

To the magic alchemy of Sunpie and the Louisiana Sunspots, who have believed in Creole music and language in Louisiana and the Caribbean for more than 20 years. To Leroy Etienne for keeping Louisiana Creole language alive. You are a living vessel, sharing language and family history in songs and stories. To Michael Harris for holding the bottom down, keeping the groove, and for singing such beautiful harmonies.

To the incredible group of special guests who came together to work with us on the songs on the album. At the New Orleans Jazz Museum, Erica Falls continued our longtime collaboration by contributing back-up vocals on "San Malo," and Ben Schenck's Panorama Brass Band performed with Sunpie on the traditional Creole song "Sali Dam." Towards the end of the project, Clarence Dalcour, Fred Johnson, and Donald "Dut" Claude's incredible singing and rhythm were solid in spirit and inspiration during the recording of the Northside Skull and Bone song "Tro Tar."

To Cayetano Hingle, our neighbor on Lapeyrouse Street and the leader of the New Birth Brass Band, for introducing the NSP to Ron Rana, the artistic director of Preservation Hall, which has led to a beautiful collaboration with the Preservation Hall Foundation, including our Creole Jazz Night live recording at the NSP. Thank you for inspiring us to think of the workshop as a place to share music and for joining us that first night.

To all the musicians who joined us in a leap of faith to record music in our corner store building: Detroit Brooks, Molly Ducoste, Louis Ford, Matt Hampsey, Joe Lastie, Kerry Lewis, and Ricky Monie.

To Rex Gregory for the great saxophone work on Leroy's songs.

To the behind-the-scenes audio engineers who helped us pull the music together: Ben Mumphrey and Jay Wesley at Studio in the Country; Tony Daigle and Steve Nails at Dockside Studios; Danny Kadar, Joe Stolarik, and Charles Butler at the New Orleans Jazz Museum at the Old U.S. Mint; and Justin Armstrong at the Neighborhood Story Project. Thank you to Mark Bingham at Piety Street Studios and Tony Daigle at Dockside Studios for mixing the songs and Paul Orofino for mastering the album.

To Francis X. Pavy for collaborating with us on the artwork for this book, and bringing San Malo to life at the Neighborhood Story Project with your lithophanes. Thank you for being an inspiration for transforming the space into a gallery, and for all the last minute painting. We loved all of it. Thank you to Cathi Pavy for the graphic design, and Arthur Roger Gallery for permission to use Francis's artwork.

To Helen A. Regis, NSP series editor, for all your support throughout the creation of this book, for helping us with French, and doing another incredible read on the book. Like songs, books have a rhythm, and you have always helped us figure out how to keep good time. To Ben Sandmel and Jeffery Darensbourg for providing feedback on later drafts. It is very reassuring to get expert opinions.

To our many friends around South Louisiana who shared their experiences with us: David Ancar, Cory Arceneaux, Big Chief Ronald "Buck" Baham of the Seventh Ward Warriors, Alvin "Pem" Broussard, Chester "Toon" Chevalier, Marion Colbert, Jeffery Darensbourg, Tony Delafose, Big Chief Clarence Dalcour of the Creole Osceola and Sandra Pichon Dalcour (we have not forgotten your delicious gumbo), Wilfred Delphin, Leo Dunn, Clarence "Jockey" Etienne, Leroy Etienne, Janet Sula Evans, Louis Ford, Rollins "Bullet" Garcia, Sr., D'Jalma Garnier, Givonna Joseph, Clayton Sampy, Jonathan and Tanya Scott, Barbara Trevigne, and Daniel Usner.

To the 219 Reed Street siblings—Bertram, Cheiron, Kerry, Michael, and Wilma—and the Payne and Alford families (aka the History Committee) for continued research and dissemination of Louisiana family history.

To important friendships in cultural institutions around the city who hosted the San Malo altar: Jay Pennington, Delaney Martin, and Alita Edgar at New Orleans Airlift's Music Box Village, Greg Lambousy at the New Orleans Jazz Museum at the Old U.S. Mint; Rollins Garcia Sr. at Bullet's Sports Bar; Sylvester, Dominique, and Robert Francis at the Backstreet

Cultural Museum; and Valerie Guillet and Lillian Cevallos at the Cultural Exchange Pavilion at the New Orleans Jazz & Heritage Festival.

To the archivists who worked with us to share important documents: Greg and Sarah Elizabeth Lambousy at the Louisiana State Museum; Sally Sinor at the Notarial Archives Division of the Clerk of Civil District Court for the Parish of Orleans; Connie Phelps and Al Kennedy with the Louisiana Collection at the University of New Orleans; Daniel Hammer and Becky Smith at The Historic New Orleans Collection, the Louisiana Research Collection, Howard-Tilton Memorial Library, Tulane University; and the Peabody Museum at Harvard University.

To important cultural centers for collaborating with us on imagery: Vermillionville in Lafayette for helping capture some of the history of language struggles in Louisiana, Tony Gradney of Slim's Y-Ki-Ki for letting us photograph his family's iconic dance hall, and New Orleans Airlift's Music Box Village for sharing photographs of their grand opening with L'Union Creole.

To the families who shared their personal archives with us: the Arceneauxs, Barnes, Dunns, and Etiennes. To John Parsons for doing the same with his collection from the Maple Leaf Bar in the 1980s.

To photographers Charles Frèger, Ed Newman, Rick Olivier, Nicola Lo Calzo, and Michel Varisco for sharing their beautiful photographs with us.

To UNO Press: Abram Himelstein and G.K. Darby for shepherding this project to publication, Chelsey Shannon for a close read as we were going through multiple drafts, and Thomas Price and Siobhán McKiernan for copy-editing.

To Charlotte Wilcox for her detective work into the bayous leading to Lake Borgne, and for transcribing many of the interviews.

To the Department of Anthropology and Sociology at the University of New Orleans for continuing to support the work of the NSP. To our fearless leader, David Beriss, and to Jeffrey David Ehrenreich, Ryan Gray, D'Lane Compton, and Francis Adeola. On the administrative side of the NSP, thank you very much to Dean Kim Long, Delinda Swanson and Emily Laan, as well as to the Office of Academic Affairs, for your help throughout all of our transitions.

To the NSP board: Helen Regis, Antoinette Jackson, Kim Long, Corlita Mahr-Spreen, Petrice Sams-Abiodun, and Troy Materre for joining us in a new era.

To Abram Himelstein, co-founder of the Neighborhood Story Project, for our years at John Mac together, and for our continuing friendship and camaraderie around book-making. To Ceirod Alexander for introducing us to Annette Street!

To Gareth Breunlin for another project blending many visions together into a seamless design, and to Kate Breunlin for sharing family time so often with these projects.

To the many participants in L'Union Creole: Dédé St. Prix, Leyla McCalla, Cedric Watson, Pascal Danae, Sully Cally, OperaCréole, and Seguenon Kone. Thank you for helping to connect the Creole diaspora through music, stories, and spirit. Thank you to Cultural Project Officer Beatrice Germaine at the French Consulate in New Orleans for believing in our collaborations. Thank you to Sully Cally for taking us to a *bèlè sware* in Fort-de-France.

To Katherine Doss, editor at *SouthWrit Large,* for publishing an early rendition of our essay on San Malo, "Pasajs/Passages for San Malo" in the spring 2017 issue on water.

To all the Louisiana Creole speakers who taught Sunpie his second language: Jockey and Leroy Etienne, Fernest and Dale Arceneaux, John and Joanne Delafose and the Delafose family, Bobby Matthews, Antoine "Fats" Domino, Danny Barker, Placide and Gerald Adams, Boozoo Chavis, Rockin' Dopsie, Sr., Martin Rodrigue, Walter DeRoche, Willie Green, Clayton Sampy, the Dardars in Breaux Bridge, the Dardars and Mamalous in Barataria, and Gilbert and Simona Creppel and the Adams family in Lafitte.

To Mardi Gras Indians in New Orleans who shared their love of Creole language and Mardi Gras Indian songs with Sunpie: Big Chief Ferdinand Bigard, Sr., of the Cheyenne Hunters, Big Chief Donald Harrison of the Guardians of the Flame, Big Chief Allison "Tootie" Montana of the Yellow Pocahontas, and the first "Chief of Chiefs," Robert Nathaniel Lee.

To Karim Brahimi (and Alliance Francaise/New Orleans). Thank you for being such a patient French teacher and answering Rachel's questions about French grammar and pronunciation.

To Laurel True and the Arts Creation Foundation for Children (George, J.R., and Resia) in Jacmel and Jacques Bartoli in Port-au-Prince for hosting Rachel's trip to Haiti in the summer of 2018. *Mèsi anpil Michou Joissaint epi Frantz "Papouche" Nicholas pou tout ede mwen pou pale kreyòl! Mèsi anpil a Fanel Leme pou anseye mwen pale ak ekri nan kreyòl.*

To the Surdna Foundation's Thriving Cultures program, which has been an incredible support for the Neighborhood Story Project's multidisciplinary/media collaborative ethnographies over the past five years.

And to our families, especially our children and godchildren, who keep our hearts growing every day. *Nouzòt lenmen twa* (We love you).

Table of Contents

Notes on Listening & Reading	1
1. In the Company of San Malo	3
San Malo | Saint Malo (Bruce Sunpie Barnes) 2:22	5
2. Languages of Power	25
3. Creole Friendship: Music in South Louisiana	49
4. Altars & Invitations	71
5. Creole Song Lyrics & English Translations	89
Hey Nom | Hey Man (Leroy Etienne) 4:22	90
Nonc Beloute | Uncle Beloute (Leroy Etienne) 3:40	92
Tristes | Sad Times (Leroy Etienne) 4:49	94
Danse Codan | Dance Codan (Traditional) 4:25	96
Shango | Shango (Bruce Sunpie Barnes) 5:30	98
Od Pour Odelia | Ode For Odelia (Leroy Etienne) 3:34	100
La Kèkenn Ape Pele Mwa | Somebody Keeps Calling Me (Leroy Etienne) 2:38	102
Bonjou Nana | Hello Girl (Leroy Etienne) 3:40	103
La Ba Che Monroe | Over by Monroe's (Bruce Sunpie Barnes) 5:55	104
Sali Dam | Salty Lady (Traditional) 5:00	105
Mo Pa Lenmen Sa | I Don't Like That (Traditional) 4:48	108
Creole Blues (Traditional) 6:36	110
Le Zonyon | The Onions (Traditional) 4:16	111
Tro Tar | Too Late (Bruce Sunpie Barnes) 2:50	112
Works Cited	114

Unidentified accordion player, circa 1850s.
Image courtesy of the Louisiana State Museum.

The Creole language['s]...genius consists in always being open, that is, perhaps, never becoming fixed except according to systems of variables that we have to imagine as much as define. Creolization carries along then into the adventure of multilingualism and into the incredible explosion of cultures. —Édouard Glissant (1997)

The problem with the idea of creolization is that it introduces nuances and subtleties, it's no longer very simple....All music from the Caribbean—from the Americas—is Creole music.
—Patrick Chamoiseau (2012)

This exploration of place and time where "creole" and "creolization" have native meaning serves to underscore the fact that some colonial cultures, particularly British North America, essentially lack these terms in their everyday vernacular, though they do not necessarily lack the equivalent cultural processes. It begs the question, "Why do some colonial cultures name the creole while others do not?" —Shannon Lee Dawdy (2000)

Notes on Listening & Reading

Le Kèr Creole is a collaborative musical ethnography that crosses time and genres to share the history and culture of Louisiana Creole. For hundreds of years in South Louisiana, lullabies were hummed, prayers were called, opera was performed, *la las* were danced, and work and carnival songs were sung in Creole. A francophone language with connections to West Africa, it is now one of the most endangered languages in the world. The United Nations Educational, Scientific and Cultural Organization's (UNESCO) *Atlas of the World's Languages in Danger* estimates only 7,000 people speak the language fluently. In South Louisiana, there are four areas where it has been well documented: around Bayou Teche in southwest Louisiana; in Pointe Coupee Parish; along the German Coast by the Mississippi River between New Orleans and Baton Rouge; and in St. Tammany Parish on Bayou Lacombe and Bayou Liberty (Valdman, Klinger, et al. 1998: 3). While New Orleans used to have the largest population of Creole speakers, very few people speak it today. However, you can still hear echoes of it in the inflection of speech, phrasing, and word choices in English.

We hope *Le Kèr Creole* will be helpful in learning how to listen to and read Louisiana Creole. We recorded the songs and wrote this companion book to share the grammar, history, politics, ethos, and music connected to the language. In a collaborative effort, we have drawn on our own ethnography in Louisiana, Haiti, and Martinique; in-depth interviews with Louisiana Creole speakers and their descendants; and an extensive literature review to situate the language and songs into broader cultural and historical contexts.

Questions about how to write the language are central to our ethnography. An oral language, Creole has rarely been written in Louisiana except to document stories and traditions associated with it. For this project, we have adopted the orthography that is the national standard in Haiti and the foundation of the *Dictionary of Louisiana Creole*—a treasure to our state, which we have consulted innumerable times (Valdman, Klinger, et al. 1998). In this orthography, every letter is attached to a sound. There are no silent letters. With a beginning understanding of how to read the vowels, you can follow along with the lyrics of the songs to tune your ear to hearing the pronunciation of the words. Here is a guide for English speakers:

s**a**   a short "o" sound like in stop

k**èk**   with or without the grave accent has a short "e" sound like in beck

s**e**   at the end of a word has a long "a" sound like in may

s**i**   a long "e" sound like in see

k**ou**ri   an "oo" sound like in cool

m**o**   a long "o" sound like in so

d**òn**   an "o" sound like on

Nasal vowel sounds in Louisiana Creole are indicated with an "n" at the end of the syllable, such as *lenmen* (to love) or *alon* (to go). Other vowel sounds are made with the use of y, as in *vyeu* (old); w, as in *bwa* (to drink); and ui, as in *nuit* (night).

This writing system diverges from French, but was developed to distinguish differences in pronunciation between the two languages. It requires a little adjustment that arrives quickly with an open mind. What does it look like in practice? For instance, French words such as *ça* (it/that) or *ici* (here) are spelled *sa* or *isi*. Other words have very different pronunciations and may diverge further from the French. Of course, even with this attempt at standardization, many difficulties arise when transcribing oral speech because, due to regional differences, there are often a number of possibilities for capturing the pronunciation of a word. This is the nature of writing a language that has not been disciplined through a school system. Louisiana Creole is still, in a sense, a *langaj maron* (wild language).

i set my light on the altar of san malo
-Brenda Marie Osbey, "In the Business of Pursuit: San Malo's Prayer"

Francis X. Pavy's "Mud Snake with Blessing." Augmented photographic lithophane in carved acrylic. Image courtesy of Arthur Roger Gallery.

1.
In the Company of San Malo

Above: Francis X. Pavy's "Blessing with Flame." Augmented photographic lithophane in carved acrylic. *Opposite Page:* Francis X. Pavy's "Bonds." Augmented photographic lithophane in carved acrylic. Images courtesy of Arthur Roger Gallery.

San Malo | Saint Malo

Lyrics, Composition, and Arrangement by Bruce Sunpie Barnes

Bruce Sunpie Barnes (*Lead Vocals and Accordion*),
Leroy Joseph Etienne (*Drums and Background Vocals*), Matthew Hampsey (*Guitar*),
Michael Harris (*Bass and Background Vocals*), Erica Falls (*Background Vocals*)

O San Malo, wiri wawiri-oh!	Oh Saint Malo, wiri wawiri-oh!
O San Malo, wiri wawiri-oh!	Oh Saint Malo, wiri wawiri-oh!
San Malo, to kache dan bwa.	Saint Malo, you hide in the woods.
Soldat, ye chase twa.	Soldiers, they hunt you.
San Malo, to vini pli mal,	Saint Malo, you are getting worse
me twa te byen plu sal.	but you've been very tough.
O San Malo, wiri wawiri-oh! [x 4]	Oh Saint Malo, wiri wawiri-oh! *[x 4]*
San Malo, to e salopri,	Saint Malo, you are a son of a bitch
me te fe de bon majik.	but you made good magic.
Lez-òt bazourdi, e pour les blon,	The others are stunned, and for the whites,
to e plu gran pri.	you are a big price.
O San Malo, wiri wawiri-oh! [x 4]	Oh Saint Malo, wiri wawiri-oh! *[x 4]*
San Malo fe gran maronaj	Saint Malo creates a big maroon village
pour libere les èsklav la ba.	to free the slaves over there.
E ye byen pase la	And they went there
pour sove se la vi.	to save themselves
O San Malo, wiri wawiri-oh! [x 4]	Oh Saint Malo, wiri wawiri-oh! *[x 4]*
San Malo to kache la.	Saint Malo, you hide there.
Soldat, ye chase twa.	Soldiers, they hunt you.
San Malo, to vini plu mal,	Saint Malo, you getting worse,
Plu gran zonbi.	the biggest spirit.
O San Malo, wiri wawiri-oh! [x 4]	Oh Saint Malo, wiri wawiri-oh! *[x 4]*

Francis X. Pavy's "Morning Mist at Colony Maron." Augmented photographic lithophane in carved acrylic. Image courtesy of Arthur Roger Gallery.

Double Fork

We open this book with a song dedicated to Juan San Malo's *gran kouraj* (great courage). His story has been told in Louisiana for centuries, and through its many tellings, we are able to learn about the language he most likely spoke: Louisiana Creole. During San Malo's time in the mid-1700s, the word Creole was used in Louisiana, as well as other parts of the Caribbean and Latin America, to identify people who traced their roots back to the other side of the Atlantic Ocean—Portugal, Spain, France, and parts of Africa—but were born in the Americas on land that belonged to indigenous people. Under these circumstances, cosmopolitan colonies developed as people lived and interacted with each other through the violence of forced labor and sex, business and love affairs, travel, and spirituality.

In the song "San Malo," a blend of Vodou rhythms connects the story of one of Louisiana's most famous maroons to music found throughout the African diaspora. The syncopation creates counterpoint rhythms to entertain the spirits. The melody calls, the bass responds. A space in between is created, but it is not empty. By not cluttering it with lyrics or notes, there is room for the spirits to enter (Cartwright 2005). Clarence "Jockey" Etienne, who was one of the most versatile drummers in Louisiana, explains what happens when you hear one of these doors open:

> It's a feeling. To get it, you got to go through it. If I can't show you by talking, I'm going to try to show you by singing. But that mostly came out of church. I would call it a deep feeling blues. You try to express yourself. You ain't hear me, now let me see if you can feel me.

The bent notes in the blues convey raw, emotional complexity. Similarly, in African-influenced languages like Creole:

> The direct statement is considered crude and unimaginative, the veiling of all contents in ever-changing paraphrase is considered the criterion of intelligence and personality. [Sidrak 1971: 6]

In Creole, a proverb may be offered as a response to a situation more than a direct reply. In the 1800s, for instance, if a person's passions had carried them into trouble, someone might have responded, "*Macaque dan calebasse*," (Monkey in the calabash), which is a reference to a fable of a monkey who puts his hand into a gourd to take a treat but cannot get it out (Hearn 1885: 23). Context is also important because words in French may take on other meanings in Creole. Nick Spitzer cites one example from his years of research in Creole-speaking communities in Louisiana:

> Monde Créole is used by community members to inclusively mean the "people of color," black Creoles or African-French Creoles, and more broadly their social and cultural aesthetics and networks. The word "monde" ("world" in standard French) translates locally as "people." [Spitzer 2003: 58]

Portraits of Odelia and Lawrence Etienne, who taught their children, including Clarence and Leroy, Louisiana Creole as their first language. Photographs courtesy of the Etienne family.

In a well-known Creole song, "'Ti Monde," (1974) Alphonse "Bois Sec" Ardoin sings: "*Oh ti monde, mo kone to dan le blues, bébé.*" (Oh, little one, I know you got the blues, baby.)

Songwriter and drummer Leroy Etienne gives another example in the use of *neg* (black). Depending on how it is being used, it can have the racist sting of the "n" word or be used, amongst Creole speaking people, as another word for person, or even a term of affection:

> I think about the word *neg*. In Creole, you can say it as a love word, and you can say it as an aggressive word, too. It's all in how you express it. When my daddy was speaking to my mother in the house, he would ask her when she is going to the store: "*Oh, Neg, to mène kèkchoz pour twa?*" (Oh, Honey, you bringing something for yourself?) He'd say *Neg* as a love word. But when he's talking about somebody back there who's crossing the property, it's not going to be the same thing. Double fork.

While a great deal of the structure of the language is based in French, Creole holds onto intonations and rhythms of West African languages as well. Leroy explains:

> Growing up between two languages, some times I thought some words were more powerful in Creole—more meaningful—because we always used it when there was something important to say in the family; it was private. When I walked in the door, my mother would say, "*Ga sa ki la! Mo ti boug vayan, rantrè, rantrè!*" (Look who's there! My fine little boy, come in, come in!) The way she said it made you feel like a king. She make me feel good. If I got hurt, my family always approached me in Creole: "*Kwa ya! To fe ton mal?*" (What happened? Did you hurt yourself?) You could feel the person cares for you in the way it was expressed.

In Louisiana Creole, people still use words that are based off of 18th-century French, like Leroy's mother's use of *boug* for boy instead of *garçon*. They also use *astèr,* instead of the more contemporary French use of *maintenant,* for "now."

Writing out these differences may take us back to places in our lives we may not have remembered in a long time—early elementary school classrooms with small desks and green chalkboards, or xeroxed foreign language worksheets and flashcards we memorized for tests. Think back to the way teachers taught you how to read and spell in English, or conversations you may have had with people who were trying to master English as a second language. How many times did an exasperated teacher end up saying, "Just memorize it!"

Why? Because the spelling of English is not consistent. The language, as we are writing it now, comes from its own process of creolization during the French occupation of England in the Middle Ages. The Middle English of Chaucer in the late 1300s was one of the first times that the hybrid language of a large French/Latin vocabulary overlaying an Old English/

An altar for Shango at Voodoo Authentica on 612 Dumaine Street in the French Quarter of New Orleans. Photograph by Bruce Sunpie Barnes.

Germanic grammar structure was written down. Nothing was standardized, and the way people communicated was in flux (see McCreum, Cran and MacNeil 1986; McWhorter 2009). Now we have rules, but the only rule in life that really plays out is change. With language, linguists could use another Louisiana Creole proverb: *Dolo toujou kouri lariviye* (adopted from Hearn 1885: 19). Water always runs to the river. "Th" sounds turn to "d"s, contractions and liaisons pull words together.

Beginning in the late 15th century, millions of Africans who crossed the Middle Passage were forced to learn to understand unfamiliar languages, including English and French. In the British colonies that eventually became the United States, the rhythm and grammar patterns of English were transformed as people began to learn to speak it, and in Louisiana, the same occurred with French. However, because of the size of the plantations and cultural differences in the way they were run, Creole diverged even more significantly than Black English, transforming into its own language (Klinger 2003).

The same disparaging comments that we hear about African American Vernacular English—that it is uneducated or "incorrect"—French speakers may say about Creole (McWhorter 2017). Clayton Sampy, who grew up speaking Creole, explains that people often think, "It's really broken down because it's a different kind of grammar." But like most sets of rules, once you get to know them they are easy to follow (see Spitzer 1986, Klinger 2003). Pronouns are a good example of how Creole diverges from French. Following is a chart of Louisiana Creole pronouns, with their French, and then English, translations next to them.

Mo: Je/I

Nuzòt: Nous/We

To, Tu, Twa: Tu/You

Vou: Vous/You formal, Y'all

Li: Il, Elle, On/He, She

Ye: Ils, Elles/They

Some of the pronouns may have connections to Kikongo in Central Africa, which uses *mono* for "I" and *ya-u* for "they." The use of gender-neutral pronouns like *li* and *ye* follow grammar rules in languages like Yoruba, Ewe, and Kikongo.

Mennen bèk (Bring back to mind) the times when you had to listen to a new language and words ran together—you weren't sure where one ended and another began. If you had to repeat them, perhaps you wouldn't know where the breaks were located. In Creole, the articles of words (*le* and *la* in French and "the" in English) are often part of a noun. For instance, in Leroy's song to his mother, *Od Pour Odelia*, he sings about a man who *pase dan lari* (passes in the road). *Lari* blends the article and noun of *la rue* together into one word. In some parts of Louisiana and the Caribbean, other Creole grammar rules have developed from West African languages such as Gbe (with its Ewe and Fon branches) and Yoruba. For definitive articles, possessives and pluralization of nouns are put at the back of the word. In other parts of Louisiana, these grammar rules are not as common. Yet, fluent speakers of Creole usually

A *ladja/danmyé* (a Martinican martial art that traces its roots to Central Africa) in Fort-de-France, Martinique on December 1, 2018. Photograph by Bruce Sunpie Barnes.

understand one another. If a Creole speaker in Haiti were to greet Leroy by saying, "*Bonjou, zanmi mwen,*" he could say back, "*Bonjou, mon ami*" (Hello, my friend.)

One of the common links between francophone Creoles in Louisiana and the Caribbean is that they do not conjugate verbs. Instead, they build out sentences with pronouns and time markers. For instance, at the beginning of Leroy's song *Hey Nonc Beloute*, he talks to his uncle in Louisiana Creole:

Mo rapel lontan pase, to te achte char, ki nwar.
(I remember a long time ago, you bought a black car.)

In this sentence, *rapel* (remember) comes from the French *rappeler* and does not need a time marker because it is in the present tense. *Achte* (buy) comes from the French *acheter* and since buying the car happened in the past, Leroy marks it with the word *te*. In Martinican Creole, however, you would need a time marker in the present tense, which is *ka*. Present progressive varies slightly around the pan-Caribbean from *ape* and *pe* in Louisiana to *ap* in places like Haiti and Martinique.

We can draw another example from Leroy's introduction to his song, *Hey Nom* (Hey Man):

Bonjou, mo pe chante pour mon padna.
(Hello, I am singing for my partner.)

In Haitian Creole, the sentence would be structured slightly differently, but speakers of both languages would most likely understand each other: *Bonjou, m'ap chante pou asosye mwen*.

Sunpie's song "Shango," dedicated to the Yoruba spirit of thunder and lightning (known as Hevieso in Vodou), calls out in different forms of Creole to honor the connections between them. The command *Vini Shango!* (Come Shango!) is used in all the forms, but in other parts of the song, Sunpie demonstrates some of the ways sentence structures diverge from each other in Martinique, Haiti, and Louisiana. For instance, you will now recognize *Nou ka danse!* (We dance!) in Martinican Creole. Later in the song, he asks Shango and his followers how they are doing:

Louisiana: *Kòman tu ye?*

Martinique: *Sa ou fe?*

Haiti: *Kijan ou ye?*

A royal deity in the Yoruba capital of Oyo (in modern-day Nigeria), throughout the African diaspora, Shango has become even more powerful, with many other *orishas* blending into his spirit (Murphy 2015: 107). Under the regimes of slavery, the West African *orishas* or *lwa* perceived to have the most power were called on for help. Here Sunpie sings in Louisiana Creole:

Spiri Afrikan,
Kouti mo kòm mo pele twa, Shango!

African spirit!
Listen to me when I call you, Shango!

Below: Master drummer and dancer Sully Cally (*back left*) participates in a *bèlè swaré* to bring in the Christmas holidays. The songs are kept in time with a *bèlè tanbou* (drum), which Sully is renowned for making by hand. Traditionally, families rotated hosting *bèlè* parties at their homes in a similar way to *la las* in Creole communities in southwest Louisiana. While the majority of people in Martinique are Catholic, connections to African heritage can be found in dancing, drumming, and singing (see Maddox 2015 for a study of *bèlè* revival in Martinique). Photograph by Bruce Sunpie Barnes.

In "San Malo," Sunpie uses another Creole word for spirit, *zonbi*. The origins of the word can be traced to *nzambi*, the Kikongo word for "soul," or "god." Throughout the diaspora, many important African words are still used in both anglophone and francophone Creoles. For instance, Louisiana and Caribbean Creoles use another Kikongo word, *bamboula*, to mean a dance to drums. In southern Kikongo, *bambula* translates as "a fetish word which magically transfers the force of external things into oneself (Wisner 2008: 47). In eastern Kikongo, *bambola* means "ignite":

Both Kikongo citations suggest the explosive and transformative. There is an associative relationship between the magical word, the power of the drum, and the transformative capacity of dance. [Wisner 2008: 47]

Another word for a dance to drums, *bele*—found in both Trinidad and Tobago, as well as other islands such as Martinique—can be traced to Central African languages as well. For instance, the Kikongo word *bwela vèlélé*, means "a dance, movements of the hips," and in the Kimbundu language in Angola, *belela* means "to dance" (68).

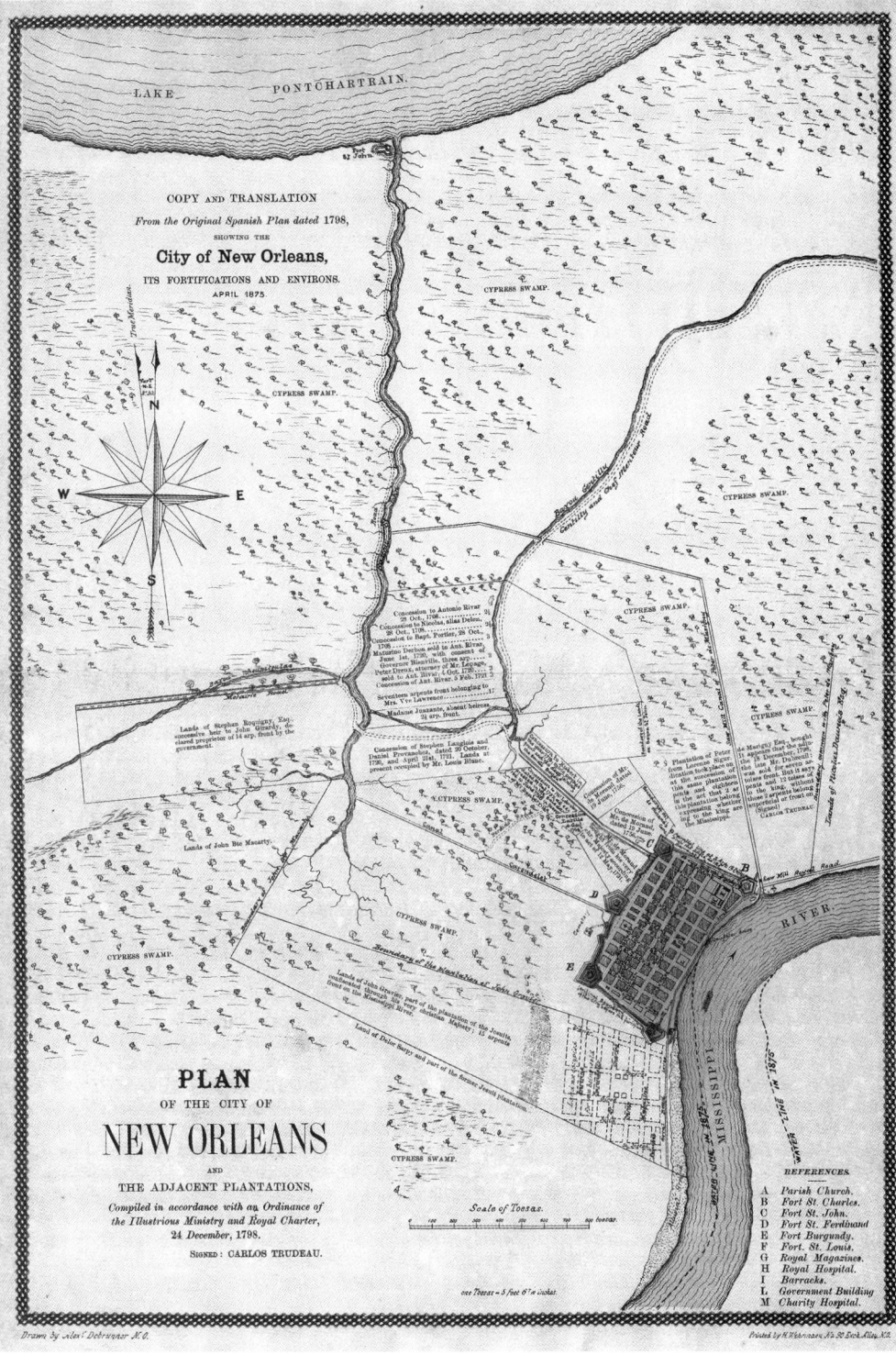

"Plan of the City of New Orleans and the Adjacent Plantations Compiled in Accordance with an Ordinance of the Illustrious Ministry and Royal Charter 24 December, 1798, signed Charles Trudeau." The LeBreton Plantation is noted on the left of Bayou Road near petite bayous like *Bayou au Lavoir* that connected to Bayou Gentilly and, eventually, Lake Borgne and the Gulf of Mexico. Map courtesy of The Historic New Orleans Collection, Gift of Boyd Cruise and Harold Schilke.

West and Central Africans in Colonial Louisiana

Who lived on plantations in colonial Louisiana? Thanks to the work of many committed historians and archaeologists, we are beginning to learn more about where people came from, and what their experiences were like (Hall 1992, Ingersoll 1996, Dawdy 2008). For instance, the meticulous research of Gwendolyn Midlo Hall and Shannon Lee Dawdy has helped us understand the lives of enslaved Africans in colonial Louisiana, including the story of San Malo. One of the important findings from Hall's research was that the majority of enslaved people originally came from the Senegambia region of Africa. Forced to raise children under incredibly difficult circumstances, they were not without power. Hall points out that in 1746, there were 3,000 people registered as "black" and only about 1,600 "white" settlers:

> Under these circumstances, Africans and Indians prevailed in many of the most crucial aspects of life. White control was relatively feeble [which enhanced] the bargaining power and self-confidence of the slaves. [Hall 1992: 77]

A watercolor, "*Desseins de Sauvages de Plusieurs Nations, 1735*" (Sketches of Savages of Various Nations, 1735), by French mason and engineer Alexandre de Batz (1685-1759) depicts a cosmopolitan market along the Mississippi River. Illinois Indians from upper Louisiana, an enslaved Fox woman (*Renarde Sauvagesse Esclave*), a child of African descent, and an Atakapa-Ishak man (*Atakapas*) from southwest Louisiana gather to trade items such as bison ribs, tallow, and bear oil. The Atakapa traveler carries a calumet, a cane river pipe used to establish new alliances or end conflict (Usner 2018; see also Darensbourg 2016 for a reflection on the painting). Watercolor courtesy of the Peabody Museum at Harvard University.

Records of the governing body of the colony, the Louisiana Superior Council, document how many slaves escaped and lived on the edge of the city where they interacted with both free people of color and whites. For instance:

> The testimony of a French sailor named Le Ber… revealed that he spent much of his time in the woods on the edge of town, "drinking with the runaways." [Dawdy 2008: 186]

Many Indian nations in Louisiana first experienced the terror of the slave trade in the 1600s when groups of Chickasaw, working with English slavers in South Carolina, began to raid villages and kidnap people to work on plantations on the Atlantic coast. When they saw Africans being forced to work on plantations along the Mississippi River, they were afraid of both displacement and bondage (Kniffen, Gregory, Stokes 1987: 65). Still, tribes living near plantations traded with European planters and enslaved Africans, and sometimes owned slaves themselves. At the time, a mixed indigenous trade language was used:

> Mobilian was a convenient second language for many settlers and slaves as well as traders to use among Indians….[T]hrough the nineteenth century it continued to be spoken by American Indians, African Americans, and European Americans in southern Louisiana and eastern Texas. [Usner 1998: 65]

Some enslaved Africans and Indians were also educated in French. The Ursulines nuns' mission in New Orleans included, for instance, "a directive to educate Indian and slave women not only to be good Christians but also to be functional literates. No evidence exists to suggest that administrators or planters ever opposed the practice" (Dawdy 2008: 59, see also Clark 2007).

During the Spanish regime in Louisiana (1762–1800), the crown's *Las Recópilaciones de los Indios* recognized the rights of Indian nations, and developed tribal policies that respected the rights of chiefs to rule over their tribes (Kniffen, Gregory, Stokes 1987: 88). Nonetheless, many slave owners were not forced to emancipate Indians they held in bondage.

In the 1780s, Spain opened Louisiana up to the international slave trade network in the Caribbean by relaxing taxes and restrictions:

> By the end of the 1780s, deliveries from the islands to the Mississippi topped one thousand per year. Jamaica, where the British declared Kingston a free port (open to foreign traders) in 1766, was the most important source for Louisiana, yet hundreds of Africans also arrived from Cuba, Dominica, Montserrat, and Saint Domingue. [O'Malley 2009: 152–154]

During the French Revolution (1789–1799), Spain outlawed the importation of slaves from the French Antilles, and planters began to rely on Kingston and Havana for slaves (see Leglaunec 2005).

A look at wills and court documents during this time gives us a view into who was living together in New Orleans. On *Chemin de Bayou* (Bayou Road), the main route in and out of New Orleans, Choctaw Indians hosted a market near *Petite Bayou au Lavoir* where they sold "furs, basketry, wild honey, beeswax, and herbs." Roots, such as sassafras, became key ingredients in Louisiana cuisine like gumbo (Kniffen, Gregory, and Stokes 1987: 95–97). Nearby was the LeBreton-Dorgenois plantation. The wills for the family estates associated with this plantation are archived on Gwendolyn Midlo Hall's *Afro-Louisiana History and Genealogy, 1719–1820* website. In 1792, 52 enslaved people are listed as part of LeBreton-Dorgenois's family estate. While the majority of people are listed as "Louisiana Creole," others are identified as Mina (as in "Elmina," on the Gold Coast in present-day Ghana through, possibly, Benin), Bamana and Mandingo (Mandé in present-day Mali), Dan (on the Ivory Coast through present-day Liberia), Yoruba (in present-day Nigeria), and Congo (in present-day Angola and the Democratic Republic of Congo). The skills of a 19-year-old man named Belly, born in Jamaica, are listed as "housekeeper, serviente, domestico." Almost all of the racial categories of the people are listed as "black," with one "grif" (a mixture of Indian and Black) and one "mulatto."

A generation later, when LeBreton-Dorgenois's son, Louis Gatien, died in 1819, the identities of the people he enslaved were more creolized. From the records we were able to access on the database, the majority of people are identified as "black" and "Louisiana Creole." One person is labeled an "English mulatto," others are "grifs" and "mulattoes." Only one, Petit Louis, a 22-year-old man from Congo, is identified by an African ethnicity, which suggests he was born in Africa.

The Louisiana Underground Railroad

Juan San Malo's early years are a mystery. We don't know his ethnicity or where he was born, but in the mid 1700s, he was living on Frederick Darensbourg's plantation in St. Charles Parish, an area where people still speak Creole today. The

River Road, which ran next to the Mississippi River, connected New Orleans to the plantations along the river. Photograph by John N. Teunisson, courtesy of the Louisiana State Museum.

plantation was next to the Mississippi River snaking wild and huge through cypress groves. Boats from the region, known as *Cote de Allemands* (German Coast) were continually leaving for New Orleans with produce (Usner 1998). When San Malo escaped, he may have hidden in one of the boats headed downriver. In the city, he could have easily learned of a series of bayous back-a-town that led to estuaries connected to the Gulf of Mexico. *Petite Bayou au Lavoir*, for instance, joined Bayou Gentilly, which wound its way through swamps to the edge of Lake Borgne in what is now St. Bernard Parish (Johnson 1992: 39; Hall 1992). By the 1780s, there are reports of San Malo and his band of maroons moving between Chef Menteur, the Rigolets, and the far ends of Lake Borgne. From there, they also traveled along the edge of the Gulf of Mexico to settlements like Bay St. Louis.

While San Malo's name has become the most well-known of the maroons, he was not alone. He had a long-term partner named Cecilia, who, according to colonial authorities, was "his inseparable companion in all his exploits" (Hall 1992: 232). Together, they became some of the earliest known underground railroad conductors, helping others escape bondage, and establishing villages on high ground created by the shell middens from Indian settlements along the edge of the lake. Children grew up without the fear of the whip. Along the bayous that wove through the area, they logged cypress trees to build homes and sold lumber to local sawmills (Hall 1992).

Landscapes from the regions where San Malo's maroon villages were located. **Top left:** A Louisiana iris, said to remind French colonizers of the *fleur de lis*, which became a symbol of New Orleans. It was also used by French authorities to brand runaway slaves. **Top right:** Palmettos next to resurrection fern growing on a live oak tree. **Bottom:** San Malo's underground railroad along Chef Menteur. Photographs by Bruce Sunpie Barnes.

In Louisiana Creole, *maron* translates as "wild" or "savage," but is often used in ways that have memories of maroonage in Louisiana. Below are examples from the *Dictionary of Louisiana Creole*. The transcription has been adjusted slightly to fit the pan-Caribbean standardization:

Ti kòne nèg va kouri maron.
You know he is going to run away.

L' ale maron dan sipriyèr. Nouzót pa konen ou l ale.
He ran away into the swamp. We don't know where he went.

[Valdman, Klingler, et al. 1998: 301]

Francis X. Pavy's "San Malo in the *Sipriyèr*." Augmented photographic lithophane in carved acrylic. Image courtesy of Arthur Roger Gallery.

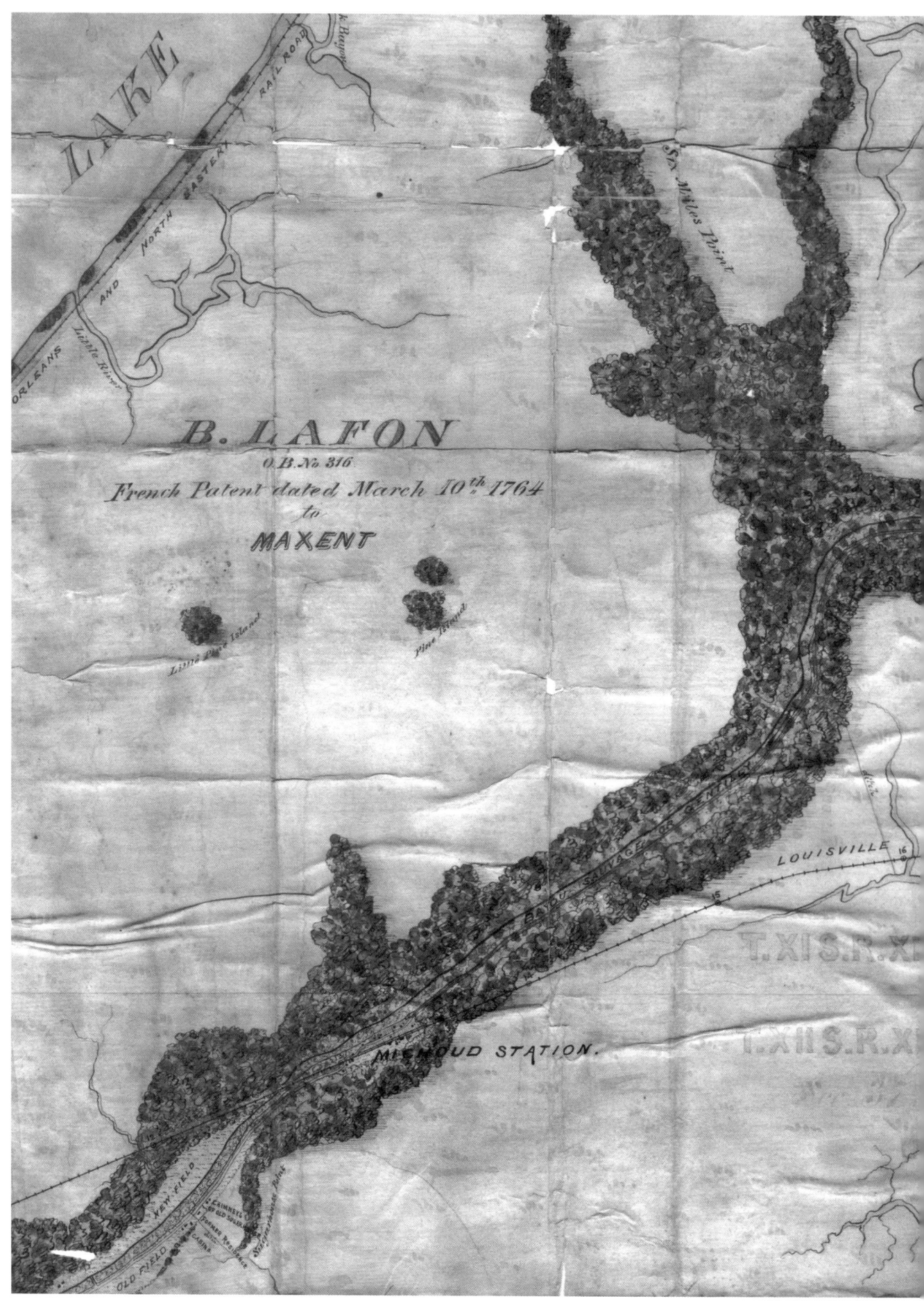

George Grandjean's "Plan of Michoud Plantation, 1883," from 8 Feb 1884, shows Bayou Gentilly leading from New Orleans to Chef Menteur and Lake Borgne. This waterway, and the high ground around it, was a central route for San Malo's band of maroons in the 1700s. Image courtesy of Chelsey Richard Napoleon, Clerk of Civil District Court and Ex-Officio Recorder, Parish of Orleans, Notarial Archives Research Center.

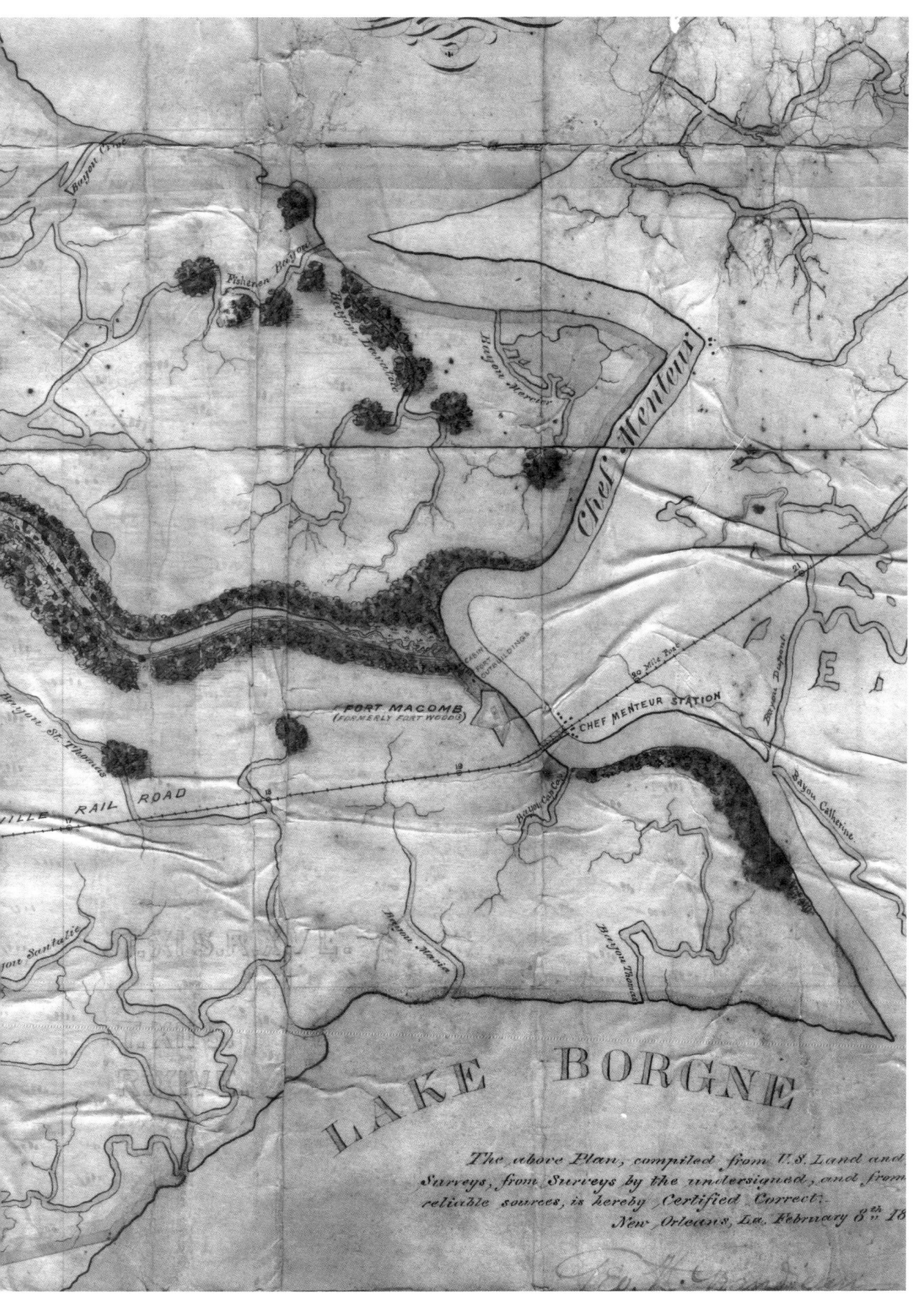

The shell midden on the edge of Lake Borgne where one of San Malo's maroon settlements is believed to have been located. Photographs by Bruce Sunpie Barnes.

Nearly a hundred years later, in the late 1800s, Lafcadio Hearn spent time with a group of Filipinos who settled in the same area. Here is his account of the sunset at San Malo Bayou:

> The bayou blushed crimson, the green of the marsh pools of the shivering reeds, of the decaying timber-work, took fairy bronze tints, and then, immense with marsh mist, the orange-vermilion face of the sun peered luridly for the last time through the tall grasses upon the bank. Night came with marvelous choruses of frogs the whole lowland throbbed and laughed with the wild music—a swamp hymn deeper and mightier than the surge sounds heard from the Rigolets bank: the world seemed to shake with it! [Hearn 2001: 90]

By the 1780s, plantation owners organized against the maroons. They pooled their money and funded militias to stalk their camps:

> Although [Lieutenant Colonel Francisco] Bouligny complained that his small force of free *pardos* (light-skinned blacks) and *morenos* (dark-skinned blacks) offered a meager challenge to the growing number of *cimarrones* (maroons) and that some of them engaged in commerce with the runaways, he and his men disrupted the band, and captured fifty of its members. [Hanger 1997:122]

Front page of one of the court cases against San Malo's band of maroons in 1783 from the Records of the Cabildo housed at the Louisiana State Museum at the Old U.S. Mint. Image courtesy of the Louisiana State Museum.

con la intencion de conducirlos a esta Ciudad y
llegado a la punta de los rigoletes en dos piraguas y saltado a tierra los americanos para
buscar leña y hacer la Cena, en este tiempo
dho negro St Malo desamarró toda la banda
los qe armados con los fuziles qe se encon-
traron descargados y St Malo tomado una
hachuela y la carabina de uno de los americanos saltaron a tierra, y el negro Jolie
Coeur le arrebato la hachuela y le rompió
+ de un yngles y
con ella la cabeza a Smalo, y luego se huye-
ron con las piraguas y bagage de los americanos y fueron a parar a la punta del
Chef Menteux estubieron tres meses los mis
mos qe duró la cura del Declarante y se
separaron de la compañia de St Malo
quedando solo el Declarante y los demas
y no volvieron a St Malo qe pasados dhos
tres meses qe volvia muchas ocasiones
a las cabañas del Declarante en compañia de otro negro nombrado Migl pertene-
ciente a Mr De Macarty en las quales
contaron al Declarante dho St Malo y
Miguel haver matado quatro Yngleses

A page from the transcript of the 1783 trial, where it is reported that Spanish colonial officials tracked maroons who were in *la compania de San Malo* (the company of St. Malo) around the Rigolets and Chef Menteur. During the Spanish colonial era, the Records of the Cabildo were written in Spanish, but day-to-day life was still conducted in French and Creole. Image courtesy of the Louisiana State Museum.

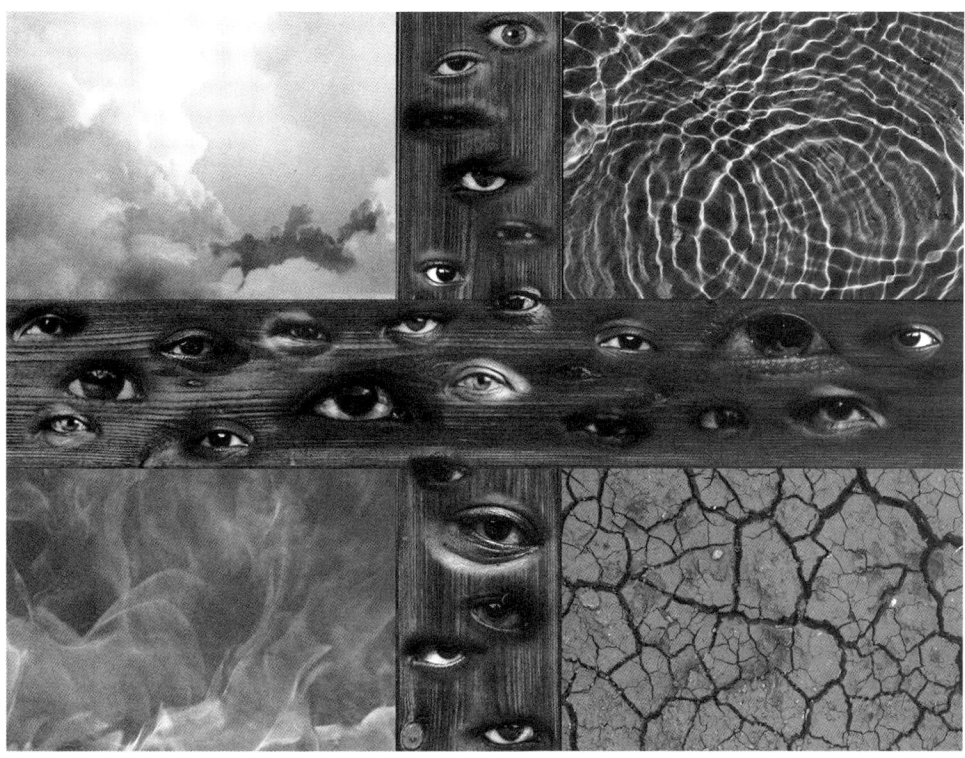

Francis X. Pavy's "Elemental Cross." Augmented photographic lithophane in carved acrylic. Image courtesy of Arthur Roger Gallery.

Records of the Cabildo document these missions along Chef Menteur and into the swamps. San Malo, Cecilia, and others were captured and brought into the city. They were accused of killing white people who had tried to apprehend them in Bay St. Louis. Yet the mindset of the colonial government went beyond specific events—all maroons deserved punishment. Their freedom provoked, if not physical, then existential uprisings. Spanish authorities said their quick inquisition led to San Malo's confession. On June 19, 1784, he was hung in *La Place d'Armes* (now Jackson Square). Cecilia said she was pregnant and avoided death, but their other companions, Joli Coeur, Michel, and Henri, were also executed, despite protests of Capuchin priests. Governor Esteban Rodriguez Miró reported that they had captured a total of 103 maroons, although there were others in the Barataria who had escaped (Hall 1992: 230). The bayous in the area around Lake Borgne—Bayou San Malo and Bayou Marron—are still named after the original maroon settlements, becoming *lieux de mémoire* (places of memory), which can lead us back to the homes they made between land and water (see Thompson 2001).

In 1792, a transcript of a court hearing of a slave revolt in Pointe Coupee Parish became the first documented record of the existence of the Creole language. The commandant in Pointe Coupee described the language in his testimony about the enslaved people involved in the uprising:

> [I]t is true that they neither understand the authentic French language nor English, but all of them understand and explain themselves perfectly in Creole which is a mixture, as I have already said, of their native language and of a poorly pronounced and structured French; which language is not known by all of the French and English citizens and inhabitants of the Province, but I, the witness, know it [Creole] very well." [Translated from the original Spanish by Ulysses S. Ricard, Jr. and quoted in Klinger 2003: 44]

Alternative Transcripts

In 1886, George Washington Cable's publication of "Creole Slave Songs" in *Century Magazine* was one of the first times Creole songs from Louisiana were shared with a broader American public (Cable 1886). Despite his research and sincere interest in the language, Cable adopted a condescending tone in his writing that was common in publications directed towards predominantly white audiences. Yet there is information in the essay that provides a window into the interconnected worlds of Creole culture and beyond. Take, for example, his thick description of Vodou practices in New Orleans, Cable writes:

> To find under his mattress an acorn hollowed out with the hair of some dead person, with four holes on four sides, and two chicken feathers drawn through them so as to cross inside the acorn.... To hear his avowed foe or rival has been pouring cheap champagne in the four corners of Congo Square at midnight when there was no moon will strike more abject fear into the heart of many a stalwart negro or melancholy quadroon than to face a leveled revolver. And it is not

Francis X. Pavy's "Birds of Prey." Augmented photographic lithophane in carved acrylic. Image courtesy of Arthur Roger Gallery.

only the colored man that holds to these practices and fears. Many a white Creole gives them credence. What wonder, when African Creoles were the nurses of many of them….[M]any a Creole—white as well as other tints—female, too, as well as male—will pay a Voodoo "monteure" to "make work," i.e. to weave a spell…made up, for the most part, of a little pound cake, some lighted candle ends, a little syrup of sugar-cane, pins, knitting-needles and a trifle of anisette. [Cable 1886: 820]

Jungian analyst Marie-Louis von Franz explains the reasoning behind the use of the material world:

[M]an is overwhelmed by ideas and concepts from within, symbols and images, but also deals with outer materials. That explains why in most rituals there is something concrete representing the symbolic meaning, for instance, a bowl of water placed in the centre for divination. [von Franz 1980: 27]

It could be the use of champagne, or it could be the conjuring of the memory of San Malo in a song or an image to help you through hard times. They have all been done in South Louisiana. Through these creative acts, *mana*, or divine electricity/energy, is connected to your intentions.

Reading the lyrics to the Creole songs included in *Century Magazine*, we have an opportunity to learn about what people considered important enough to sing about—what resonated with them. Their songs remembered "*pitis sans popa, pitis sans moman*" (children without a father, children without a mother) and shared the voice of runaway slaves who taunt Spanish colonial officials saying, "*C'est vrai, yé*

pas ca-pab pran moin!" (It's true, they can't catch me!) One longer song, "Ourrá St. Malo" (Dirge for San Malo), was collected from an older woman from St. Bernard Parish named Madeline. In her song, San Malo's story is told again. This time, the maroon stands strong with his people:

> Yé mandé li qui so comperes.
> Pov St. Malo pas di' a-rien!
>
> *They ask him who his comrades are.*
> *Poor St. Malo says not a word!* [Cable 1886: 814]

It is San Malo's last act of resistance before he loses his life. The power of the song went up against the court records to hold onto a different version of history. An important repository of cultural memory, music continues to travel through time, keeping names and stories alive that other institutions and archives suppress. As Clarence "Jockey" Etienne said about the innovations he made in Creole music throughout the 20th century:

> Oh, they try to stop me now. Oh, they tried to barricade me many times. Now I have to figure you trying to barricade me because you didn't get there. Cause loneliness coming. Don't bring me with you. I ain't going. I'm telling you now. You get mad if you want to; that's up to you. That's your decision.

Portrait of Odelia Porter Etienne, Leroy and Clarence's mother, in St. Martin Parish, Louisiana in the early 20th century. Photography courtesy of the Etienne family.

2.
Languages of Power

Left: Jazz musician and historian Danny Barker. Photograph courtesy of the Louisiana State Museum. *Right:* Barker's childhood home on Chartres Street in the French Quarter of New Orleans was just a block away from St. Mary's Catholic Church. Photograph by Bruce Sunpie Barnes.

An Underground Language

In the early 20th century, musician and historian Danny Barker was growing up on Chartres Street in the French Quarter of New Orleans, which he called "the Creole section" of the city. Although a small boy, he was attuned to the way that the humidity in the nighttime air helped the sound of the riverboat calliopes find their way into his bedroom. He paid attention to the routes and cries of the street vendors, and recognized how a funeral parlor's tips on who had just died helped his family's brass band prepare for parades. He also recognized that the songs of his neighborhood were sung "top to bottom in French and Patois:"

> These songs were full of spirit and had a beat, and on Mardi Gras Day, you would hear groups of maskers singing in Creole Patois and dancing the Bombouche (Bom-bu-shay)....I heard these songs all over the neighborhood. Catholic Creole women doing housework and nursing their babies sing these songs. [Barker 1998: 91]

Barker's reflections echo the work of Ngugi wa Thiong'o, who writes in *Decolonising the Mind* about the importance of one's childhood language:

> Our appreciation of the suggestive magical power of language was reinforced by the games we played with words through riddles, proverbs, transpositions of syllables, or through nonsensical but musically arranged words. So we learnt the music of our language on top of the content. The language, through images and symbols, gave us a view of the world, but it had a beauty of its own. [Thiong'o 1997: 11]

As a young boy, Barker began his formal education at Medard Hillaire Nelson's private school in the French Quarter. A Creole of African, French, and Choctaw ancestry with roots in the West Indies, Nelson grew up in a devout Catholic family and attended St. Mary Catholic Church where he was an altar server. Close ties to the church eventually led him to travel to Rome, Paris, and London to study languages and become a priest. When his parents were fatally struck by lightning in their home, he returned to Louisiana. Nelson took care of his 12 brothers and sisters and opened his school at 1218 Burgundy Street. His great-grandson describes the student body:

> With his education and command of seven languages... His school was open to all, blacks, whites, Indians, Italian immigrants, students from the islands, rich and poor. [Lagarde 1989: 48]

Nelson taught courses in English, French, and Spanish; his expertise was sought out in the creation of Xavier University. He was at the epicenter of education, at the crossroads of many cultures. His students were expected to come dressed formally: "The boys who could not afford a *cravat* were given a string to put around his neck as a substitute for a necktie" (Arceneaux quoted in Dawdy 2000: 138). An avid gardener, he grew pomegranate, fig, and peach trees in his courtyard and covered its walls with grape vines, which "provided both food and shelter from the summer sun" (138).

One day, Barker recalls walking past his teacher during recess and hearing him complain, "The people in this city do not speak the real French language, it is a bastard language they speak" (Barker 1998: 94).

Left: St. Mary's Catholic Church on Chartres Street in the French Quarter, where Medard Hilaire Nelson was an altar server. Photograph by Bruce Sunpie Barnes. *Right:* Portrait of Medard Hilaire Nelson, courtesy of the Orleans Parish School Board Archive at the Louisiana Collection, University of New Orleans.

In this small exchange, in a private school that went against the grain of society in so many ways, we get a chance to glimpse the difficulties of holding onto Creole. While there are not many other written accounts of how Creole was handled in educational settings in Louisiana, we can look to school systems in other parts of the Caribbean for possible analogies. For instance, in Haiti, where the vast majority of the population speaks Creole, French is thought to be a hard language to learn. Creole linguist Albert Valdman quotes a proverb, "*Kreyòl pale, kreyòl konprann*" (What is expressed in Creole is clear) to explain that French is often "associated with duplicity and obfuscation" (Valdman 1988: xii). Similar feelings of class distinction have been part of the history of teaching French in Martinique. Patrick Chamoiseau, one of the great theorists of the poetics of Creole languages, wrote a memoir, *School Days,* to share some of his own experiences learning French. Here he takes us back to his first initiations:

> Baffled, the little black boy realized that he did not know this language. The chatty lil' voice in his head used a different language, his home language, his Mama-language, the language he had not learned but rather absorbed with ease as he eagerly explored his world....really speaking—to say something, give vent to an emotion, express yourself, think things over, talk for any length of time—required the Mama-tongue that (ayayayaye!) was proving useless in school. And so dangerous. [Chamoiseau 1997: 48]

As Chamoiseau joins his classmates in learning French, their enthusiasm is often crushed when their teacher ridicules their pronunciation of words. In this scene, they are shown a piece of fruit:

> Reaching into a bag, he pulled out an *ananas* [pineapple] and carefully placed it on the class register.
> "What is this fruit called?" ...
> A hearty cry burst from the congregation.
> "A *zanana*, messie!"
> Horrors.
> The teacher gulped. His face was contorted with anguish. His eyes became glittering stones. Zounds!... However do you expect to trravel [sic] along the path to wisdom with a language like that? This po-nigger talk gums up your minds with its worthless pap! [Chamoiseau 1997: 60–61]

The teacher's intense reaction to the differences in pronunciation between Creole and French deserves a little linguistic detour into the differences in the way that French is written and spoken. The "z" sound, for instance, is not captured in writing, but comes from a "liaison" that occurs in speaking when the plural article *les* is put in front of a noun that begins with a vowel. The written "s" that is put at the end of a noun to indicate it is plural is not spoken. Thus, one would write "the pineapples" in French as *les ananas*, but would pronounce the words as *le zanana*. Of course, as West Africans were originally trying to understand French, they knew they had also heard a "z" sound, so they attached it to the noun: *zanana*.

Similar decisions were made in Louisiana, as we can see in the case of a song on *Le Kèr Creole*, "*Le Zonyon*," (The Onions), which is taken from street vendor calls in New Orleans. To follow the logic, we return to the French *les oignons*. According to the rules of spoken French, a "z" sound will be created between the words and the "s" will not be pronounced; thus the noun *zonyon*. Knowing the differences in languages helps us understand how choices have been made; they make sense. However, many teachers do not openly discuss where the disconnects between the written and spoken French come from, which is one of the reasons the language is considered to be so hard to learn as a second language. (The same, of course, applies to English. Take a minute to consider all the uses of French silent letters, as well as the differences in pronunciation of words, in this text.)

In places where Creole is spoken as a home language, it is often relegated to a second-class position. Cècile Accilien explains this linguistic hierarchy in Haiti:

> [S]peaking French usually indicates money and power. It is also an indication of the speaker's literacy—their need to "show off" by speaking French. People who don't speak French as treated as inferior. [Accilien 2007: 79]

Within these class distinctions, Creole speakers often look upon French warily:

> There is popular Haitian maxim that contrasts [Haitian Creole] HC with French as *lang achte*—literally, a "bought language," a language that is rather inaccessible and that is often obtained, "bought," at great psychological and socioeconomic costs. In discussing the notion of *lang achte* as applied to French, Valdman (1984:82) aptly compares HC to the Vodou believer's *lwa rasin*, the Vodou spirits that are part of one's family heritage; these are the "native" spirits, so to speak, on a par with the native language. In this metaphorical context, French would be the linguistic counterpart of the *lwa achte*, the nonnative spirits that are sometimes bought at a burdensome price from the Vodou priest. It is generally advised that one stay away from these unsympathetic *lwa achte*, who often make costly demands that overwhelm the Vodouisant's modest means....HC [is] a mother tongue that need not be bought. Indeed HC is effortlessly acquired by all Haitians. [Degraff 2005: 570]

Medard H. Nelson had acquired all the power of the *lang achte*. He taught a multiracial student body in a city where black education had been systematically disenfranchised, yet he apparently did not see worth in the language of many of his students. Did he force a double consciousness on them for their survival, or was he deaf to the beauty of the language surrounding him? We return to Chamoiseau, who writes of what he gained from his education in French:

> To you, dear Teacher, I owe my loving regard for books. Thanks to your reverence of them, they will always be alive for me. You handled them delicately, you opened them with respect. You closed each one as though it were a book of prayer. You put them away with a jeweler's care.

Yet he doesn't forget those who resisted the teacher's scorched language policy, and calls out those who left school to stay in their mother tongue:

> I'm grateful...for your underground language. You fled through it, took refuge in it, resisted with it, inhabited it with infinite familiarity, and this fierce deep rootedness endowed your language with a latent strength whose combustive power I would realize only many years later. [Chamoiseau 1997: 128-129]

Chamoiseau's generation (b. 1953) was the first to embrace the possibilities of writing in this mother tongue. For generations before, the Creole language was often written by white court reporters, journalists, and folklorists who transcribed songs and stories (see Kein 2000). These days, most people in Louisiana are not aware of the exact laws that were passed to formally prevent French from being spoken, nor are they aware of the substantial differences in the multiple forms of French spoken in south Louisiana. In *Le Kèr Creole*, we would like to go back in time to understand how Louisiana Creole has become one of the most endangered languages in the world. There are many moments where we could begin, but we will choose 1803, the year of the Louisiana Purchase. Napoleon Bonaparte's military had invaded Haiti in an attempt to re-establish slavery after the successful revolution. Repelled, the emperor decided that without the profits from its former sugar colony, France did not want its North American real estate at all (Kulka 2004).

The Generation After

It had only been a few years since France had reclaimed Louisiana from Spain. At the time, the entire population of lower Louisiana was only 37,000, with the majority of people living in New Orleans and surrounding plantations. During the Spanish colonial era, court documents were written in Spanish, but French still prevailed in business and education. With the American takeover, this arrangement was no longer a guarantee. Jefferson's appointment of William C. C. Claiborne as the first territorial governor, who spoke neither French nor Spanish, signaled a lack of cultural respect for the local population. On January 2, 1804, *Moniteur de la Louisiane*, "reported that Creoles sobbed openly in frustration and despair while the French flag was lowered for the last time on the *Place d'Armes*" (Needham 2002: 67). Without citizenship rights that accompanied statehood, Louisianans knew they were facing a foreign occupation.

A few days after the transfer of power, Claiborne attended a Creole ball as a sign of good faith. He must have been told music and dancing were central to Louisiana's social world, but was shocked when a dispute around language and music arose. Below is a translation of Pierre Clement de Laussat's account of what happened when a French quadrille began to play:

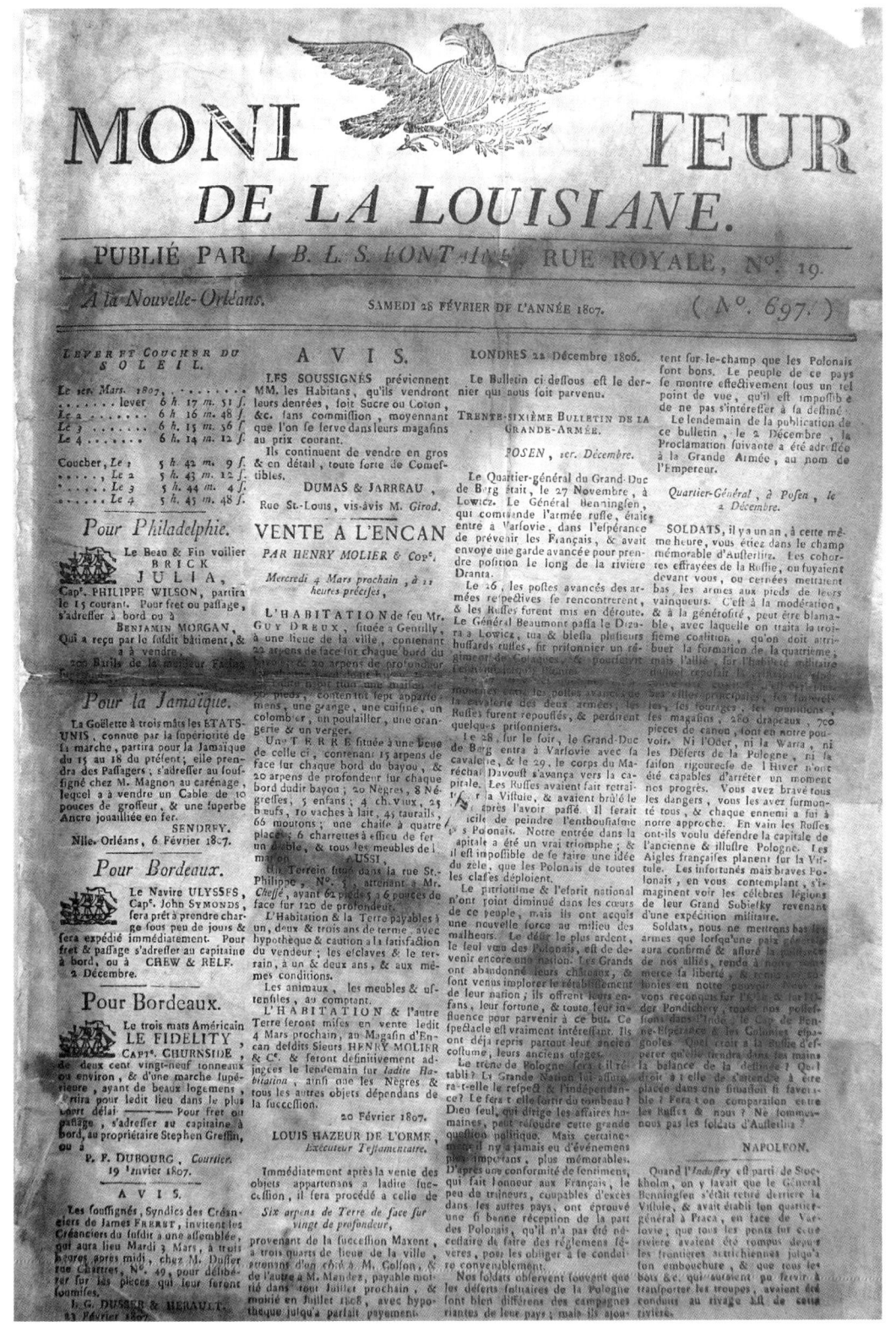

The front page of *Moniteur de la Louisiane* from February 28, 1807. Founded in 1793 by an immigrant from Saint-Domingue, Louis Duclos, its office on Royal Street in the French Quarter was the sole source of journalism in New Orleans until the Louisiana Purchase. In 1797, another immigrant, Jean-Baptiste Le Sueur Fontaine, became *Moniteur*'s editor. This page from 1807 includes advertisements for ship departures to Philadelphia, Jamaica, and France, as well as auctions of property that list the number of slaves and animals that are for sale. Mr. Guy Dreux's property, located on one of the bayous, includes a list of horses, oxen, milk cows, as well as *"20 Negres, 8 Negreffes, 5 enfans"* (20 Black men, 8 Black women, 5 children). Image courtesy of the Louisiana State Museum.

Other publications in Louisiana that were published by Saint-Domingue refugees include Claudius Belurgey's *Le Télegraphe* (1803 to 1812), Hilaire Leclerc and later Arnold Du Bourg's *L'Ami des Lois* (1809 to the early 1820s), Francois Delaup's *L'Abeille* (formed in 1827), J.B. Theirry and Dacqueny's *Le Courrier de la Louisiane*, and Daudet's *La Lanterne Magique* (see Dessens 2007: 141).

Kanaval (Carnival) in Jacmel, Haiti. On the streets of the city, different cultural organizations perform traditional dances. Photograph by Fedno Lubin.

An American, taking exception, brandished his stick over a fiddler, and there was at once, great turmoil.... The French quadrille was allowed to go on, but the American interrupted it on its second time around with an English quadrille, taking his position on the floor; someone cried out: "If the women have a drop of French blood in their veins, they will not give in!" [Needham 2002: 69]

Soon afterwards, the City Council wrote an ordinance which specified the order of French *contredanses*, English country dances, and waltzes (favorites of the Spanish) at public balls (Needham 2002: 70). As the city grew over the next decade, so did its love of music. At least 30 public ballrooms and private homes hosted dances almost every night:

Balls would begin at eight o'clock or else directly after the opera performances at the opera house itself. They continued through the night, halted at three o'clock for an earthy breakfast (such as gumbo and venison) and would shut down operations when dawn interrupted to spoil the fun. [Needham 2002: 68]

The wealth and leisure of the elite was largely tied to the plantation economy. When the U.S. Congress banned slave ships from foreign ports coming into Louisiana, a group that included two major sugarcane planters went to Washington to ask for the ban to be lifted and to continue to allow the use of French in government and courts (Russell 1999: 396). A few months later, slave trading was allowed to resume with the stipulation that ships would come in through Charleston, South Carolina. This arrangement was short lived. In 1808, the United States banned the international slave trade (Leglaunec 2005: 227). Soon afterwards, the City Council in New Orleans passed police codes that prohibited enslaved people from attending balls given by free people of color and put a curfew on all people of African descent. Two years later, it "ordered the police and watchmen to patrol the streets, public squares, and levees at dusk and arrest vagrants and runaways as well as disperse all gatherings of enslaved people" (Evans 2011: 139). A Creole saying arose from the laws:

Après yé tiré canon,
Nègue sans passe, c'est nègue-marron

After they fire the cannon,
A black without a pass is a maroon.

Lafcadio Hearn explains in *Gombo Zhebes*, "This referred to the old custom in New Orleans of firing a cannon at eight P.M. in winter and nine P.M. in summer, as a warning to all slaves to retire....Any slave found abroad after these hours without a pass was liable to arrest and a whipping of twenty-five lashes" (Hearn 1885: 16). Increasingly, laws were shaped by American concepts of racial inequality, but many of them were difficult to enforce as the city's population continued to grow and change with the domestic slave trade, immigration, and the arrival of refugees from the Haitian Revolution who had been kicked out of Cuba. This mass migration between May of 1809 and January 1810 nearly doubled the size of New Orleans and changed the culture of the region in significant ways (LaChance 1992: 105). White refugees who had been part of the planter class in Saint-Domingue aligned themselves with the white Creole population in the city. Following the lead of the publishers of *Moniteur*, they launched a new wave of publications that ensured that French would continue to be spoken in the city and surrounding parishes. In 1812, the Louisiana State Constitution made a concession to the language as well:

> [L]aws passed by the state legislature must be made available in the language of the Constitution of the United States, i.e., in English, but that provision recognized that the ordinary language of public affairs was French. [Bell 2008: 43]

The new francophone immigrants also included a large free people of color population with a strong commitment to equal rights, as well as enslaved people who spoke a different form of Creole. Eight years after the Saint-Domingue refugees arrived, Louisiana was publishing 33 French-language newspapers and journals throughout the state (Picone 1997: 122). In the countryside and in the downtown neighborhoods of New Orleans, most people did not speak English at all.

Mass Displacement

Governor C.C. Claiborne's decision to allow enslaved people from the Caribbean to enter the state after the ban on the international slave trade was highly unusual; a concession to the French-speaking planters of South Louisiana. In the years that followed, the majority of traffic in human beings came from the domestic slave trade in Virginia and South Carolina. Between the 1820s and 1830s, the population of enslaved people in New Orleans doubled. William Bell Brown, who had been enslaved in Missouri, wrote a memoir of traveling through the South at this time:

> The tearing asunder of husbands and wives, of parents and children, and the gangs of men and women chained together, en route for New Orleans market, furnished newspaper correspondence with items that never wanted readers....many of the slaves were as white as those who offered them for sale, and the close resemblance of the victims to the trader, often reminded the purchaser that the same blood coursed through the veins of both. [Brown 1880:107]

Purchased by both French-and English-speaking households, the new arrivals found themselves in a state divided by language. English, as the growing language of power, was seen as an asset amongst Creole-speaking slaves. In 1831, for instance, a refugee from Saint-Domingue complained that "everywhere one only hears English spoken, for in every house there are a number of old servants who have become fluent in this idiom" (LaChance 1992: 119). Upon arrival, the *Amerikans* used to the institutions of slavery in the upper South would have encountered a society with a much larger free people of color population. Shannon Lee Dawdy suggests Louisiana's development of a three-tiered racial structure is connected to differences in French and Anglo-American religious worldviews. Still embedded in ideologies of white supremacy, the Catholic, francophone community viewed relationships across race differently than Protestant, anglophone ones:

> That a culture's ideas about sex may be intimately tied to its ideas about race makes both sociological and cosmological sense. To create a new race through a sexual act is to admit to a probably sinful liaison. In the Catholic world-view, this sin is forgivable in the privacy of the confessional and a place is found for the children produced by these unions. In the Protestant world view, the sin may mean eternal damnation; at the very least it means a scarlet letter and social castigation. The risk is too grave, so their existence is denied. [Dawdy 2000: 121]

Dawdy's thesis is given weight by Protestant clergy's strong support of the American Colonization Society, a national organization that promoted a "back to Africa" movement to send free black people to a newly formed colony in Liberia. At its core, the organization "sought to eliminate the contradictions of American democracy brought on by the presence of Negro slaves" (Reilly 2002: 434). The contradiction was based on their belief that people of African descent were not, and would never be, equal to those who were permitted into white society. In South Louisiana, the strongest proponent of colonization was the Presbyterian planter from Baltimore, John McDonogh, who devised a work plan for people enslaved on his plantation, McDonoghville, to purchase their freedom:

> All freed slaves on the McDonogh plantation had to agree to emigrate to Liberia, for in the master's view blacks and whites could not possibly live together as equals. One or the other race would prevail. The vanquished faced extermination. McDonogh was convinced this was nature's law. [Reilly 2002: 447]

Letter from freed slave Galloway Smith McDonogh to his former owner John McDonogh. As part of John McDonogh's belief in the "Protestant work ethic," he set up a system on his plantation where people could purchase their freedom over a 15-year period if they agreed to move to the colony of Liberia. Galloway Smith McDonogh settled in Sinoe, Liberia, and sent this letter back asking about his love, Fanny, whom he hoped to marry. He later returned to the United States. "Galloway Smith letter, 1842 June 1. Page 1" in JohnMcDonogh Papers. Letters from former slaves, 1842–1845; Manuscripts Collection 30, Boxes 11–12. Louisiana Research Collection, Howard-Tilton Memorial Library, Tulane University.

McDonogh's position of radical inequality reflected the sentiments of many white settlers who saw the removal of freed blacks as part of the American colonization of the Ohio Valley and Louisiana. Presidents James Madison, Henry Clay, and Andrew Jackson were all a part of the society. However, McDonogh diverged from others in his support of black education. On his plantation, he employed a black pastor who taught people who were working towards their freedom how to read, claiming to those who questioned the decision that he "could not always be on the watch to prevent them from violating the law" (quoted in Cornelius 199: 168). It was his commitment to education that helped to endow both New Orleans and Baltimore public schools after his death in 1850 (see Devore and Logdson 1991).

In the spring of 1829, Andrew Jackson became the seventh president of the United States. A slave-owner in Tennessee, he built his military reputation by waging war against the Muskagee (Creek) Nation in Alabama. At the Battle of Horse Shoe Bend in 1814, his troops:

> surrounded eight hundred Creeks and killed almost all of them, including the women and children. Afterward, his soldiers made bridle reins from strips of skin taken from the corpses; they also cut off the tip of each dead Indian's nose for body count. [Takaki 1993: 85]

Jackson himself bragged that "I have on all occasions preserved the scalps of my killed" (1993: 85). From Alabama, he went on to defeat the British in the Battle of New Orleans. As president, he pushed Congress to pass the Indian Removal Act (Takaki 1993: 85; Ortiz-Dunbar 2014: 96), which forced Indian nations on the eastern side of the Mississippi River to move to reservations in "Indian Country." The Louisiana Purchase treaty had stipulated that the United States respect Indian sovereignty. However:

> rapid encroachment by an expanding plantation society and the government's promotion of that expansion relentlessly weakened Indian control over their lands and resources. [Usner 2018: 42]

By the late 1830s, the Louisiana legislature passed laws that prohibited interracial "conspiracy" and denied the legitimacy of "mixed race" children, which prevented them from inheriting property from either one of their parents (Bell 1997: 18). Many Indians of mixed descent were also classified under the categories of "colored" (Jolivétte 2007).

Creole Resistance

In a review of Black education in Louisiana during the 1800s, Paul A. Kunkel explains:

In cultural opportunity, the Negro whether free or slave, was severely curtailed at least by the letter of the law. In general, his education in Louisiana was legally prohibited…However, many of them did receive good formal training. Free people of color attended schools in Louisiana surreptitiously conducted, or, if wealthy, attended institutions in France. Others were educated by religious orders of the Catholic Church. The law, generally, tacitly tolerated these efforts…if it did not disturb established orders—if it did, the courts took forcible action. [Kunkel 1959: 6-7]

Despite the Constitution of the United State's guarantee of freedom of the press, censorship was overtly legislated. The state of Louisiana enacted a law that prohibited printed material that had "a tendency to produce discontent among the free coloured population…or to excite insubordination among the slaves" (Bell 1997: 18). A judge could decide how harshly to enforce the law, which ranged from three to 21 years of hard labor or even the death penalty.

Free people of color and their allies realized it was safer to write in French, which directed publications to audiences with a history of greater tolerance than the growing anglophone population (Blassingame 1973: 134). In the 1840s, J.L. Marciacq published the first journal of African American writing in the United States, *L'Album Littéraire: Journal des jeunes gens*. Although short-lived, it included an anonymous article protesting the censorship of the free black population (Brosman 2013: 72). In 1845, Armand Lanusse edited the collection of Romantic poetry by people of color, *Les Cenelles: choix de poésies indigènes*. Many of the contributors were also community organizers and educators who helped establish the *institut catholique des orphelins indigents*, or Couvent Institute—a Catholic school open to orphaned children of color (Dedunes 1973). Marie Bernard Couvent was born in West Africa. As a young girl, she was kidnapped and brought to Saint-Domingue before most likely moving to Louisiana after the Haitian Revolution. She married a free man of color who was a carpenter. Although she did not learn to read and write, when she passed, she bequeathed her estate to open the institute. In 1866, Harper's *New Monthly Magazine* (Willey 1866) reported on the school. Keith Weldon Medley summarizes some of the details:

Students were taught in French and English. Boys and girls studied on separate floors. Until 1900, report cards contained individual progress evaluations rather than grades. The school community raised money through solicitations, festivals, firework displays, Carnival balls, and raffles of lace work, umbrellas, and holy pictures. [Medley 2014: 70]

The tolerance of the school seems to have been related to its francophone roots in the Creole part of New Orleans. When John Francis Cook, a wealthy African American civil rights advocate from Washington, D.C., attempted to open a school for "free Negroes" in New Orleans, he was forced to leave the city for defying the law (Kunkel 1959:6).

According to historian Caryn Cossé Bell, in the ten years after the founding of Couvent, laws were written to prevent

"free negroes and mulattoes" from entering the state, required slaveholders to remove emancipated slaves from Louisiana within 30 days of their manumission, and finally, in 1857, prohibited slave emancipations altogether. Other laws prohibited interracial marriages; restricted free black access to public accommodation; barred free black children from attending public schools; prohibited free blacks from serving on juries, and required free persons of African descent to carry identification papers. [Bell 1997: 87]

Catholic parishes in Louisiana had been integrated, but the new laws supported segregation in churches. In St. Martinville, for instance, trustees at St. Martin de Tours began implementing separate seating, and imposed a hierarchy in the order of who received communion: first whites, then free people of color, and lastly enslaved people (Alberts 199: 84). In parts of New Orleans, parishioners resisted the inequality. During the Civil War, the priest at St. Rose de Lima on Bayou Road, Father Claude Paschal Maistre, opposed the Archdiocese's support of the Confederacy. Members of his congregation, *La Société des Fleurs de Marie,* took money raised at mass that was supposed to be sent to Confederate soldiers and gave it to the Couvent school instead:

By Lent of 1862, Father Maistre spoke out on the contradiction between Catholic teaching on equality and the actions of church officials in support of the Confederate causes, one of which was slavery. Maistre thereby distanced himself from the hierarchy's pro-slavery stance and attempted to promote black political equality in his parish. [Alberts 1998: 111–113]

The organizing was regularly written about in *L'Union*, the first newspaper published by people of color outside of the Northern states (Foner 1988: 63), and drew anger from the Archdiocese. When the Vatican did not reprimand the congregation, the Archdiocese shut the church down in 1864.

St. Rose de Lima was ahead of its time. After the Civil War, Louisiana's state charter in 1868 required officials to recognize, by oath, the equality of all men. Of all the Reconstruction constitutions in the South, it was the only one to explicitly require equal treatment in public accommodations, including equal access to public schools (Foner 1988, Bell 1997: 21). In New Orleans, Anglo-American members of the school board, as well as other European immigrant leaders, opposed a restoration of bilingual education that had been common before the War. One member, E.C. Kelly, said, "our Public Schools were established for the purpose of giving a thorough common school English education and nothing

Left: Architectural design for St. Rose de Lima, named after the first Catholic saint canonized in the Americas. Born Isabel de Flores in Lima, Peru, in 1586, St. Rose never married. In her 20s, she joined the Third Order of St. Dominic in Lima and devoted the remaining years of her short life to prayer and the care of children and the elderly. At the time of her death in 1617, she was described as a "Creole woman from this city" (Graziano 2004: 104). In the early 1900s, *The Picayune's Guide to New Orleans* wrote, "On Bayou Road, between North Dorgenois and North Broad, is a beautiful little church…The congregation is exclusively French" (*Picayune* 1904).

Right: Before Hurricane Katrina, Givonna Joseph (*left*) was the musical director at St. Rose de Lima for five years. With her daughter, Aria Mason (*right*), she founded OperaCréole. The opera company is dedicated to researching and performing lost or rarely performed works by composers of African descent, with a specialty in 19th century New Orleans free composers of color. They also write their own operas, including *Les Lions de la Reconstruction*, which tells the story of Father Maistre and the congregation at St. Rose de Lima. Photograph by Nicola Lo Calzo.

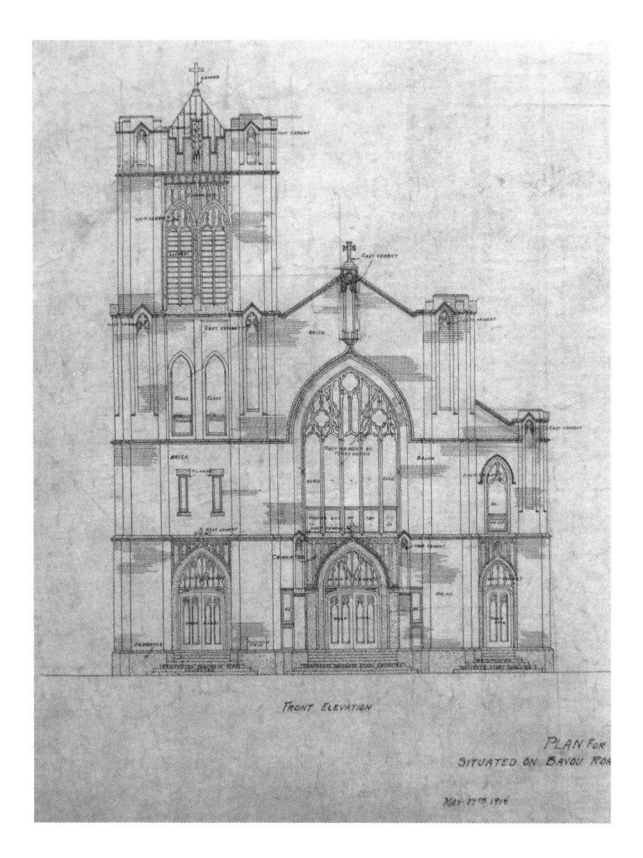

more" (Devore and Logdson 1991: 63–64). As a compromise, French was taught as a required subject, but not as the main language of instruction (Estaville 1990: 109).

During Reconstruction, public schools in Creole neighborhoods of downtown New Orleans were the first to integrate, and the Couvent Institute's former teachers and students were "among the chief leaders in the movement" (Devore and Logdson 1991: 42). By the mid 1870s, George Washington Cable reported on John McDonogh's namesake, an all-girls school in the French Quarter:

> I saw, to my great and rapid edification…children and youth of both races standing in the same classes and giving each other peaceable, friendly, effective competition. [Devore and Logdson 1991:73]

Yet, the instruction of English had an impact on South Louisianans' feelings about Creole. Lafcadio Hearn reported around the same time:

> Education is slowly but surely stifling the idiom. The younger colored generation is proud of its correct French and public-school English, and one must now seek out the older inhabitants of the Carré in order to hear the songs of other days, or the fables which delighted the children of the old régime. Happily, all the "colored Creoles" are not insensible to the charm of their maternal dialect, nor abashed when the invading Amerikain superciliously terms it "Gombo." There are mothers who still teach their children the songs—heirlooms of melody resonant with fetish words—threads of tune strung with gris gris from the Ivory Coast. [Hearn 2001: 38]

Writing Creole

As people of color gained more political power, the Creole language was used by the francophone media to misrepresent newly elected officials of African descent as uneducated. In the early 1870s, for instance, the journal *Le Carillon* (The Alarm Bell) protested the gains in civil rights by stereotyping black politicians in Creole (Thompson 2001: 248). The editor, Forester Durel, portrayed C. C. Antoine, the lieutenant governor of the state, as an "orangutan" speaking "gumbo" as a way to argue he was unfit to govern (Dominguez 1994, Jordan and DeCaro 1996: 57).

Throughout the years, *Le Carillon* easily code switched between French and Creole because its readership—white Creoles from South Louisiana—were fluent in both languages. Raised by Creole-speaking servants, caregivers, and family members, they were also familiar with the language's poetics (Hall 1992: 194). For instance, when George Washington Cable collected Creole songs from antebellum Louisiana, "Ah Suzette" was recorded in a "Creole drawing-room in the Rue Esplanade." Its lyrics indicate that it most likely came from a song brought to Louisiana by an enslaved person from Saint-Domingue after the revolution, but was being played by an upper-class white Creole family:

M'ale-lè haut montagne, zamie.
M'ale-lè coupe canne, zamie.

I'm going to the high mountain, friend.
I'm going to cut sugarcane, friend.

[Cable 1886: 824–825]

"Creole Slave Songs" was not the first time Cable had written about white Creoles' use of the Creole language for a broader national audience. In the opening chapter of his novel, *The Grandissimes* (1877), English readers are introduced to a *bal masqué* (masked ball) set in New Orleans just after the Louisiana Purchase. We meet Old Agricola Fusilier, a white Creole patriarch, who is asked by another masker: "*Comment to yé, Citoyen Agricola?*" (Cable 1957: 2).

Fusilier chuckles in understanding (How are your people, Citizen Agricola?). If the reader is unclear about what just happened, Cable jumps back into the narration to note that the speaker has the "familiarity of using the slave dialect."

The masked character continues in Creole, "*Ah! mo piti fils, to pas connais to zancestres?*" (Ah, my little son, you don't know your ancestors?) Writing with a French orthography, Cable shifts parts of the sentence to show the differences in Creole. *Mo* replaces *mon* for "my," *petit* becomes *piti*, and the "z" sound that Patrick Chamoiseau's teacher tried so hard to rid his students of comes through in the pronunciation of *ancestres*. In this short dialogue, Cable shared a language that had connected black and white Louisianans together for generations—not to lampoon them, but to show their intimacy.

Published just a few years after the withdrawal of federal troops and the end of Reconstruction, many white Creoles condemned Cable for fear that readers "would get the impression that Creoles were not of unsullied white descent" (Tinker 1953: 215). A priest named Adrien Rouquette, who grew up on Royal Street in the French Quarter and later lived across Lake Pontchartrain ministering to Choctaw villages, wrote a poem denouncing the book. In it, he implies it is Cable who is up to miscegenation. While practicing "Negro-Vodouism," he may also be having an affair with "*bel nègrésse* [sic] or the vodou queen Marie Laveau" (Brosman 2013: 100). Yet in Roquette's critique of *The Grandissimes*, he also shares how familiar he is with Creole. Literary historian Gavin Jones notes the irony:

[R]ather than extricating the author, and implicitly the White-Creole population of New Orleans, from the "crimes" attributed to Cable—namely, a familiarity with and a participation in African-American culture—this poem suggests both the knowledge of and the willingness to adopt black creative forms. [Jones 1999: 126]

The same year *The Grandissimes* came out, Louisiana writer Alfred Mercier published a reflection on his own experiences with Creole. Mercier was raised on his family's plantation in Jefferson Parish near New Orleans and said Creole was his first language, the one he learned from the enslaved people who took care of him. He said he favored it more than French so much that his parents conspired to make him stop:

Je me souviens de la récompense qui me fut accordé, le jour où je m'engageai envers mes parents à ne leur parler désormais que le français.

I remember the reward given to me the day I promised my parents to thereafter only speak to them in French.

[Mercier 1880: 378, translated in Gipson 2016: 462]

However, Mercier not only continued to speak Creole, he began to write it, claiming that people needed to take it on its own terms—not other standards. He wrote, "*Il se prête au récit, il excelle dans le conte*" (It lends itself to narration, it excels in the tale) and claimed that Homer's epics could be fully translated into Creole (quoted in Gipson 2016: 470). He became one of the first writers to give the language serious attention as scholarship (Brosman 2013).

A Metaphor for the Future?

Two years after the U.S. Supreme Court's 1896 verdict in *Plessy v. Ferguson*'s legalized segregation in the United States, the Democrats in the Louisiana Congress organized a constitutional convention under the leadership of E.B. Kruttschnitt, the nephew of Judah Benjamin, who had been Secretary of State of the Confederacy. His primary goals as president of the convention were to eliminate the rights of black voters and to change the mandate for universal public education, arguing that, "every man shall have the power to educate himself if he so desires" (Devore and Logdson 2011: 114). On February 8, 1898, he opened the Louisiana Constitutional Convention:

St. Pierre, Martinique with Mt. Pelée in the background in November of 2018. Photograph by Bruce Sunpie Barnes.

We know that this convention has been called together by the people of the state to eliminate from the electorate the mass of corrupt and illiterate voters who have degraded our politics. [quoted in Kunkel 1959: 17]

Black voter registration went from 154,000 to 500, and public education for black students was eliminated except from the first to fifth grades (Devore and Logdson 117–118). In 1910, the city had 68 white public schools and only 16 colored ones. Until 1917 (when McDonogh 35 was established), there was no high school for colored students. Linguist Thomas Klinger points out that the disenfranchisement was even more extreme in rural areas. In 1901 in Pointe Coupee Parish:

> Reverend Pierre LaForet Albert Plantvigne founded the Industrial and High School for blacks in the town of Oscar, on False River...Two years later he was gunned down by a white resident for this transgression of the region's unspoken code against educating the descendents of slaves. [Klinger 2003: 122]

In 1906, E.B. Kruttschnitt died unexpectedly and the *Times Picayune* lamented the loss of a leader who "Secured White Supremacy in State." A few months later, the City of New Orleans declared the small park near *Petite Bayou au Lavoir* on Bayou Road, just down the street from St. Rose de Lima, "Kruttschnitt Place."

The white supremacist agenda of the Louisiana legislature was mirrored in the development of the Louisiana Association of the American Folk-Lore Society. The organization was founded by Alcée Fortier (1856–1914), an educator and historian who was born in St. James Parish to a family who traced their roots to River Road sugarcane plantations. His book, *Customs and Dialects* (1894), provides a window into his opinion of the people he studied:

> The negroes, as all ignorant people, are very superstitious. The celebrated sect of the Voudoux, of which so much has been said, was the best proof of the credulity and superstition of the Blacks, as well as of the barbarity of their nature....how the Creoles fear the Voudoux! [Fortier 1894: 129–131, quoted in Jordan and DeCaro 1996: 40]

Fortier's research was publicly disputed by Lafcadio Hearn, who believed that Louisiana Creole culture could be a "metaphor for America's future" rather than being an exotic "place apart" (Bronner 2005: 145). He also argued that Vodou needed to be respected as part of a dynamic hybridization of religious beliefs brought from Africa and transformed in the Americas (172). During his lifetime, Hearn was not an academic, nor an institution builder. It was Fortier who trained another generation of white folklorists to use their direct connections to plantation communities to "collect" folklore in ways that promoted inequality (Jordan and de Caro 1996, see also Gipson 2016: 461). Yet the quality of Hearn's work has stood the test of time and has shaped the way that New Orleanians see their city (Starr 2001). It has also been an important reference for literary movements in the Caribbean. As novelist and literary critic Gayl Jones has written:

One of Anabelle Guerrero's "*Les Pierrotines*" (Women of St. Pierre), a public art project commissioned by Patrick Chamoiseau as part of the Grand St. Pierre Project to support the culture and art of the region. Guerrero worked with archives to share historical photographs of women from the first capital of Martinique with residents of the city. Some of the most in-depth research on St. Pierre before Mount Pelée's eruption in 1902 came from the work of Lafcadio Hearn. Photograph by Bruce Sunpie Barnes.

To liberate their voices from the tyrannic frame of another's outlook, many world literatures continue to look to their own folklores and oral modes for forms, themes, tastes, concepts of symmetry, time, space, detail, and human values. [Jones 1991: 192]

Martinican writers such as Édouard Glissant and Patrick Chamoiseau, who started the creolité literary movement, identified Lafcadio Hearn's folklore collections as important contributions to decolonizing literature in the Caribbean. Beginning in the 1940s with Aimé Cesaire's journal, *Tropiques*, writers have drawn on Hearn's nuanced transcriptions of spoken Creole to develop new rhythms in their writing (Bongie 1997: 154).

In Louisiana, scholars have addressed the misrepresentations of Marie Laveau in the historical record (Ward 2004, Fandrich 2005, Long 2006). After all the sensationalist accounts, West and Central African spiritual practices continue to be infused in Catholic rituals that are more quietly passed on through families. Barbara Trevigne, a genealogist who grew up in a Creole-speaking family in the Seventh Ward, has been writing about how her community's traditions are connected to them:

All persons who are Catholic don't necessarily practice the same rituals in Catholicism. We have different rituals here than a lot of Catholics have somewhere else. We're founded on the Latin Catholic, and because of

Janet Sula Evans, a Mami Wata priestess who was initiated in Accra, Ghana, lights frankincense in front of an altar that students in Rachel Breunlin and Bruce Sunpie Barnes's Public Culture course at the University of New Orleans created at Kruttschnitt Place to share the history of Bayou Road and to consider the legacies of segregation that we are still living with. Photograph by Bruce Sunpie Barnes.

Sula's maternal line traces their roots in Louisiana to the matriarch of the Creole community in Natchiotches, Marie Therese Coin-Coin. Sula's shrine, the Temple of Light Ilé de Coin-Coin, is dedicated to Marie Therese. Part of Sula's work in New Orleans has been helping people reconnect to their ancestors and West African traditions. She teaches about the four elements to include on an ancestral altar: water (preferably from a body of water important to you), air (represented by incense or one's own breath to send prayers to the divine), fire (candles to connect to the sacred light inside of you), and earth (dirt, stone, or crystals from sacred and/or ancestral land). She explains you can make an altar on a table or on the ground. From these basic elements, you can add flowers, photographs of the dead, objects that remind you of them, offerings they may have enjoyed like tobacco and fruit, and libations.

Barbara Trevigne's altar dedicated to her ancestors at her home in the Seventh Ward of New Orleans in 2018. Photograph by Bruce Sunpie Barnes.

the influence of West Africa and those slaves bringing with them the cultural memory of their religion. I remember the May crowning at St. Mary's Academy when it was in the French Quarter. Your parents pledge you to the Virgin Mary so she can always protect you. Very Catholic, very traditional. We would take a wreath of flowers and put it on the Virgin Mary.

Leroy's cousin, Dennis Williams, who grew up in St. Martinville, remembers how he became connected to her:

> [W]hen I was eight or nine, I asked Mama why she used to dress me in blue and white…She told me that those were the colors of the Virgin Mary, and that one day the doctor told me I wasn't going to make it. On that day she sold me to the saints. [Tisserand 1998: 184]

Barbara explains how these Catholic traditions seemed normal to her:

> When I got older, and ventured a little further out of the community, I realized that everybody didn't have a religious altar in the home. We always had an altar, and there were always candles burning with pictures of saints and ancestors.
>
> While we were very Catholic at home, we also talked about Hoodoo. And I always heard of Marie Laveau. It wasn't anything to be afraid of—it was embraced.

And it's more or less incorporating those elements together. I always heard, "Oh girl, you look just like Marie Laveau" because I liked hoop earrings. Matter of fact, my grandmother used to play Marie's numbers in the lottery: 3, 7, and 11.

In her essay, "Holding It Together, Falling Apart," Rebecca Snedeker writes about how African spirituality has been embedded in the city:

> I was raised in a Episcopal church and school, but my spirituality, my understanding of the world and how it works, is distinctly New Orleanian, which means it is also African. The African idea of *gris-gris*, or fetish— the old idea that an object has a soul or anima—is normal here. I collected acorns and magnolia pods, bits of the outdoors that carry the key to a tree, and grouped them with special objects like the porcelain figurines that my grandmother passed on to me. Although I didn't call them altars at the time, that's what they were. [Snedeker 2013: 142]

The blending of Christianity and African religions began on the other side of the Atlantic, where art historian Donald Constentio reminds us, "Cruficixes, rosaries, plaster images of the saints…were assimilated by Africans in Dahomey and Kongo before the Middle Passage" (Cosentino 1995: 30). The ability to embrace other traditions is part of a cosmopolitan ethos:

Left and Right: In A. E. Washburn's "1896 Topographical Map of Morehouse Parish, Louisiana," a "general revision of old maps," the winding bayous and oxbows near the Mississippi River are a defining part of a countryside divided by plantations. On the left, the Alford plantation, where Bruce Sunpie Barnes's family worked as sharecroppers in the 1920s, can be seen towards the bottom. On the right, plantations owned by the Daniel family, who were targeted by the Ku Klux Klan, are shown towards the bottom. Map courtesy of the Library of Congress. *Middle*: Bruce Sunpie Barnes's grandmother, Margaret Moore's brother, John Lee Moore, in Morehouse Parish at the turn of the 20th century. Photograph courtesy of the Barnes family.

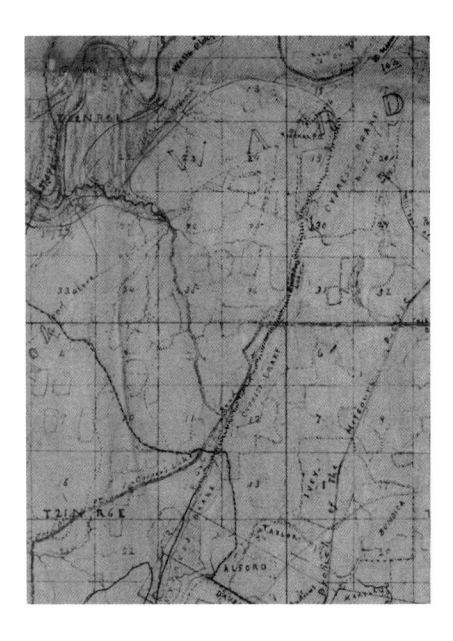

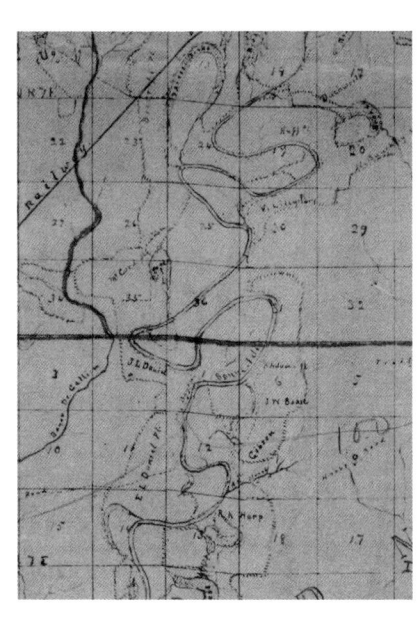

Vodun does not refuse Christianity, rather it welcomes Jesus as another Vodun spirit. Incorporating and embracing foreign elements…into its global constitution and on its own terms ensures Vodun's ongoing… survival. [Rush 2013: 21]

English Only

The United States has never adopted an official national language. Throughout the conquest of Indian nations, the transatlantic slave trade; immigrations from all over the world; the purchase of Louisiana, the conquest of Tejas, New Mexico, and Alta California; and the colonization of islands such as Hawaii, the Philippines, Samoa, and Puerto Rico, English has never been written into the Constitution. Yet, it is undoubtedly in charge. At the beginning of the 20th century, Theodore Roosevelt sounded like Orleans Parish School Board representatives when he announced there was "room for one language in this country and this is the English language, for we must assure that the crucible produces Americans and not some polyglot boarding house" (quoted in Picone 1997: 36).

While New Orleans was still one of the most cosmopolitan cities in the United States, since the Civil War, Louisiana had become 70 percent Anglo-American, with most of the population settling in the northern part of the state (Picone 1997: 122). In 1916, when school became mandatory, the Board of Education required courses to be taught in English.

In the midst of World War I, anti-immigrant sentiments in the U.S. intensified when the Russian Revolution overthrew the Tsar in 1917. Once again, revolution ignited the imagination of people in Europe and the Americas. Yet there was a strong backlash. In the early 1920s, the Ku Klux Klan reconvened as an organization committed to white supremacy that was defined as "100% Americanism…white, native-born, fundamentalist Protestant values, including Prohibition and sexual probity" (Hair 1991: 127, see also Brown 2006). Throughout the United States, millions of people became chartered members. Extending out of the South, some of the largest memberships were in Indiana and Oregon. The Klan's anti-Catholic stance made the organization relatively unpopular in southern Louisiana, but in the northern part of the state, it became a political force.

On the Louisiana-Arkansas border in the late 1800s, Morehouse Parish had the most lynchings per capita of any parish in the state. In Bastrop, the Klan developed a strong base with J.K. Skipwith, a member of the Klan during Reconstruction, taking on the role of "exalted cyclops." His branch targeted "disorderly people" who lived "irregular lives": bootleggers, moonshiners, immoral women and men who, in Skipwith's words, "associated with niggers" (Hair 1991: 131). Not far away, the white men in the town of Mer Rouge mostly refused to participate, with a well-to-do planter, J.L. Daniel, and friends openly confronting the organization (Alexander 1965: 69).

In 1921, a group of 50 black-hooded, masked Klansmen stopped cars going towards Mer Rouge to look for Daniel's son, Watt. A veteran of World War I and graduate of Louisiana State University, Watt was well-loved by the community. He also lived with a black woman and sold alcohol. When the Klan pulled the Daniels' car over, they beat J.L. and another

100 LINES I WILL NOT SPEAK FRENCH ON THE SCHOOL GROUNDS 1916–1968

An exhibition at Vermilionville, a living history museum in Lafayette, Louisiana, recreates a classroom where students were forced to write, "I will not speak French on school grounds" after the Louisiana state legislature passed a law outlawing the use of French in public schools in 1921 (see Natsis 1999: 326). At the very bottom is a small act of resistance, drifting back into writing the same words in French: *Je ne parlerai pas francais a l'ecole*. Photograph by Bruce Sunpie Barnes.

man before letting them go. Watt and his friend, Thomas F. Richardson, never came home. Their bodies were found in Lake Lafourche a few months later. Their bones were broken. Their hands and feet had been cut off, their testicles smashed (Hair 1991).

The terrorism in Morehouse caused a state crisis, and the governor, John M. Parker, found his loyalties split. His family owned plantations in Mississippi, but he was raised in New Orleans. In 1874, his father fought in the Battle of Liberty Place, an attempt by the White League to overthrow the integrated government during Reconstruction (see Wagner 2004), and he had been one of the organizers of the lynching of Sicilians at the Orleans Parish Prison after the murder of the New Orleans police chief, David C. Hennessy. But the Klan's terrorism against white men apparently had gone too far. Married to a Catholic woman from the city, with his daughter enrolled in a convent school, he wrote to the federal government for help.

The exalted cyclops's response was defiant, declaring in a Klan newspaper that Parker was "lined up with the most depraved nigger lovers the South has ever known" (Hair 1991: 133). The Klan put tombstones on the lawn of the governor's mansion in Baton Rouge (Alexander 1965: 71). The national guard was brought into Morehouse Parish to mediate between Bastrop and Mer Rouge. No one was ever charged with the murders.

In August of 1921, Louisiana state legislature outlawed French as a language of instruction in schools. A month later, to curtail Klan activity, Governor Parker promoted a bill prohibiting masking except on Mardi Gras. Senator Jules Dreyfous, an immigrant from Alsace-Lorraine who represented New Iberia in southwest Louisiana, introduced it on September 28, 1921, by declaring he was "100% American and 100% Jew" (Brown 2006: 165). It is telling that he did not include his first language, undoubtedly a blend of French and German, as part of what it meant to be a Louisianan. Students were now punished for speaking any form of French in schools:

> Virtually every elderly French speaker in rural and semi-rural Louisiana can recite the cruel and humiliating details of the continued implementation of this policing. In many homes, French became a secret language for parent-to-parent communication. The future of any language is obviously undermined whenever the language's chief value for parents is that their own children don't understand it." [Picone 1997: 123]

The phenomenon has been studied around the world. In *Languages in Competition: Dominance, Diversity, and Decline*, Ronald Wardhaugh identifies one of the keys to keeping a language alive as "openness":

Creole-speaking jazz musicians in New Orleans: Louis "Big Eye" Nelson Delisle, George Murphy "Pops" Foster, Paul Barbarin, Sidney Bechet, Albert Glenny, and Alphonse Picou. Photograph by Al Rose, courtesy of the New Orleans Jazz Museum at the Old U.S. Mint.

> When a language is "open," it becomes more readily available to potential speakers and can expand...[In Louisiana], the social stigma engendered an inferiority complex among speakers. [Brown 1993: 71]

During the 1920s, the Archdiocese began to support racial segregation of Catholic churches throughout Louisiana, which created even deeper divisions in language and culture. While black parishioners had continually resisted the second-class statuse they were given in their home parishes, most thought dividing congregations would only reinforce racism. However, with very limited opportunities for schooling, when the Archdiocese proposed creating "colored schools" in newly segregated parishes, others saw the change as an opportunity for self-determination (see Fairclough 1995: 14, Dubois and Melancon 2000: 244). In the Seventh Ward of New Orleans, Corpus Christi opened for black Catholics in 1914. With 12,000 members, it claimed to be the largest black Catholic church in the world.

The trend towards the segregation of Catholic churches also censored French. St. Ann's, an integrated parish in the Sixth Ward with services in French, was segregated into the newly formed St. Peter Claver in the 1920s with services in English (Estes 2000). Mother Katharine Drexel and her order of nuns, the Sisters of the Blessed Sacrament, funded the creation of segregated "colored" churches with parochial schools in southwest Louisiana. Clayton Sampy, who grew up in Our Lady of Assumption, explains what his early education was like:

> I started going to school there. It was hard for me because my parents didn't know how to read; they couldn't teach me. And when I was going to school, I was talking Creole, not English. I had a hard time over there. The nuns told me not to talk French. But I learned; I started speaking English.

Barabara Trevigne, who was born in New Orleans around the same time as Clayton, shares her family's story:

> I grew up across A.P. Tureaud in a double shotgun house. My mother and my three siblings lived on one side, and my grandmother, my uncles, and my cousin Andre lived on the other side. My grandmothers spoke Creole. Neither one taught it to us because they were made to feel that it contributed to bad English. Some of the nouns, the verbs, you know, they would say 'at' for 'hat.' They spoke it within their family, to their sisters, and especially when they didn't want us to know. And remember, when they were little, they were discouraged from speaking it in school. You know, "No, you speak English." The Americans dominate.

Who Is Creole?

In the 1930s and '40s, Alan Lomax traveled across southwest Louisiana and parts of the Caribbean recording Creole music for the Library of Congress (Szwed 2010). In 1950, he decided to write a biography of Ferdinand "Jelly Roll" Morton, one of the first jazz pianists to come out of New Orleans. Lomax considered Morton to be one of the great storytellers of his era, "an intellectual and a wit," as well as a fantastic composer and improviser. Lomax described him as a "Creole of mixed, lower-class origins," and outlined his point of view:

> [He] understood his music was also a Creole gumbo of African, French and Spanish Creole, Mississippi black, middle American, with a touch of American Indian. He perceived that jazz was the product and

resolution of painful class tensions between "lower" American blacks and "upper" French-speaking mulattoes. [Lomax 2001: xvi]

In the 1890s, Rodolphe Lucien Dedunes discussed some of these tensions when he wrote, "Some Creoles in our own day have fallen to such a point of moral weakness that they have disowned and rejected not only their fellow blacks but even their own kin" (Desdunes 1973: 18). George Murphy "Pops" Foster, who was raised on Henry McCall Plantation in Ascension Parish before moving to uptown New Orleans, wrote in his autobiography:

> The worst Jim Crow around New Orleans was what the colored did to themselves. The downtown clubs and societies were the strictest. You had to be a doctor or a lawyer to get in. The lighter you were, the better they thought you were. The Francs Amis Hall was like that. The places was so dicey that they wouldn't let us come off the bandstand because we were too dark. [Foster and Stoddard 1971: 65]

In addition to discrimination, during Jim Crow segregation, lighter-skinned people sometimes took advantage of being able to cross color barriers to sit at the front of the bus or go into a store. Ronald "Buck" Baham explains functional passing:

> Sometimes they still call them *passé blanc* because you have some blacks from the Seventh Ward who are real, real light. Light eyes. Years and years ago, they could go in different stores where blacks wasn't allowed, but through the back door.

Others crossed over more permanently. Foster tells a story of his cousin's infiltration of the white musicians' union:

> Dave Perkins was the president of it. They didn't know he was colored. He played tuba and trombone and taught music and lent out instruments. He played with all the white bands. [Foster and Stoddard 1971: 62]

In these stories, the false pretenses of essential difference assumed in the boundaries of white supremacy are broken down. Yet in associating Creole identity with light-skinned privilege, many New Orleanians and scholars from around the world forgot that Creole, as a language, is not confined to one particular part of the city, or one skin color. For instance, in *Subversive Sounds: Race and the Birth of Jazz*, Charles B. Hersch writes:

> Black musicians and bands with few or no Creoles identified themselves as Creole as a defense against racism or to create a more respectable image, as in [King] Oliver's "Creole Jazz Band." [Hersch 2007: 97]

Joseph Nathan Oliver was born in Edgard, Louisiana in 1885, which in located along the Mississippi River in St. John the Baptist Parish (Hahn 2008: 57). In the late 19th century, the majority of people coming off the plantations in this parish would have spoken Creole. Joe was raised by his half-sister in uptown New Orleans after his parents died, but most likely would have retained his knowledge of the language—an important social currency in the city with other musicians. In the 1910s, he co-led a band with Kid Ory, a Creole-speaking musician from the Woodlawn Plantation around Donaldsonville in the same parish where Oliver was born (McCusker 2012:10). Ory, whose father's side of the family were Alsatians from the German Coast, could have passed for white, but lived on Jackson Avenue in the heart of Central City, and played with musicians like Louis Armstrong and Pops Foster. Unfortunately, many early jazz historians did not speak French or Creole, and in the oral histories they conducted, there is only a cursory mention of musicians speaking "French." Still, New Orleans musicians continued to record songs in Creole through the mid-20th century.

Holding On, Letting Go

In 1968, the state of Louisiana ended its directly adversarial relationship with French and passed a bill that allowed the language to be taught in public elementary and high schools again. The state legislature also created the Council for the Development of French in Louisiana (CODOFIL), sponsoring radio and television programs in French, festivals, bilingual publications, and exchanges (Picone 1997: 124), as well as hiring teachers from France, Belgium, Quebec, and parts of the Caribbean. Trained in teaching standard French, many of these international teachers did not understand the differences between Creole and other varieties of French in Louisiana. It soon became clear that more groundwork would have to be done. After more than 40 years without any formal instruction in reading and writing in French, most French speakers in Louisiana wrote only in English. Linguist Michael Picone outlines the dilemma educators were facing:

> Should the written code be regularized and brought closer to the prevailing international standard or should it be authentic for the region even if that means resorting to innovative written constructions and spellings to capture the divergences? [Picone 1997: 142]

Barry Ancelet, a scholar and activist who has been part of the movement to revitalize the French language, has written about the history of reintroducing French in public schools. In the 1970s, "representatives of CODOFIL were reluctant to consider the notion of incorporating the local variety in the classroom." He quotes CODOFIL President James Domengeaux:

> Why should we perpetuate illiteracy in the classroom by teaching Cajun French? It's an oral language. It doesn't have grammar. It doesn't have a written form. [Ancelet 2007: 1245]

Top: Leo Dunn's great-grandmother, Ernestine Torregano, who spoke Creole to his mother.

Bottom: Leo Dunn, on the left, with his family as a young boy. Photographs courtesy of the Dunn family.

been less active in the city than in other parts of the state. Perhaps one of the reasons is because the Creole language is often conflated with other cultural and racial politics (see Tregle 1992). During the Black Power movement, many people associated Creole identity with light skin privilege (see Spitzer 1986). David Ancar, whose family spoke Creole, shares his experience growing up in New Orleans with "bright" skin:

> It's hard to try to explain this to you, but I'm gonna try. Growing up as a kid, people were angry with me because I looked like this. I've got straight hair, but I have no control over this. I tried to blow dry my hair into an Afro. That didn't go so well. My daughter's mother was from the Magnolia Projects, and black people in that area would think I'm white. I understood their reaction. I would bite the bullet because I knew we had bars here in the Seventh Ward where some darker people couldn't get in.

To separate themselves from these institutions, many people whose family spoke Creole distanced themselves from the Creole cultural identity (see Spitzer 1986, Hirsch 2007, Breunlin and Regis 2009). Leo Dunn explains his own family's decisions to embrace solidarity with Black culture:

> I grew up in the Seventh Ward and attended Corpus Christi Catholic Church. My mother, Audrey Millon, was mostly raised by her great-grandmother, Ernestine Torregano, whose first language was Creole. She grew up speaking it, too. Even though the language was important to my mother's side of the family, we didn't identify as Creole. My father always told us we were Black. He remembered times when light-skinned Creoles didn't speak to him at school, when he couldn't go into the Autocrat Club. He taught me to stand with Black people of all colors who have had to struggle in Louisiana, and in the United States.

Outside evaluations commissioned by CODOFIL recommended a "Louisianification" of French education in the state because the program may have "inadvertently done as much harm as good by discounting the value of Cajun and Creole French" (Ancelet 2007: 1246). A proposal to adopt a textbook, Donald Faulk's *Cajun French* (1977), which used an orthography written for English readers, was made and was almost adopted by the Louisiana Board of Elementary and Secondary Education. However, many scholars worried writing this way would cut off the language from the larger Francophone world (Brown 1993, Nattis 1999, Ancelet 2007). It also did not account for the other forms of French spoken in Louisiana, such as Creole (Spitzer 1986: 139).

Even though New Orleans used to be one of the largest areas of French and Creole speakers in Louisiana, CODOFIL has

Poet Mona Lisa Saloy often writes about growing up in the Seventh Ward with a family who defied color prejudice. In her poem "My Mother's the Daughter of a Slave," she takes us back to the beginning of the 20th century:

> an early generation of free city-Black women,
> New Orleans, 1907,

Marion Colbert, the Queen of the Banana Trees, next to St. Augustine Catholic Church in Tremé. Ms. Marion's grew up in the Seventh Ward of New Orleans with Creole-speaking parents. Photograph by Bruce Sunpie Barnes.

when jazz honked and tonked dives
in the Vieux Carré and uptown.
She was jet-black, and she was happy.
Never knew she was cute
"'til a high yellow nigger named Louie came 'round
Called Mother pretty black, almond eyes,
streetlight bright.
I never knew her grown.
She said, "Live good, bébé."

[Saloy 2005: 11]

Mona Lisa's mother died when she was still young, and she was raised by her father who spoke Creole. Marion Colbert grew up in the same neighborhood as Mona Lisa's father. The values she has lived by reflect a Creole ethos:

I was raised with Creole people. That's all they used to talk—more Creole than the English. My father, Charles Smith, was a plasterer. My mother, Annie Larose, was a housewife. We belonged to Corpus Christi Catholic Church. My mother didn't go in bars, but on Sundays, she used to like to play two cent pitty-pat with her friends. She made anisette (liquor made with anise seeds popular in France) with different colors like red or green, and homemade vanilla ice cream for us children. Once a month, they had dances at the church—the cake walk. My mother loved that. She would wear the long dresses with the ruffles, and a big bow in her hair.

When I was seven years old, she took sick. I could remember my mother was in the bed. Her hands were spread far from her body, and my father was holding her, looking down, and talking to her. At two o'clock in the morning, they brought her to the hospital and she passed. She left six children—four boys and two girls.

My mother's oldest sister lived right next door to us in a house my grandfather had built. My father said, "I can't raise girls," and he did not want nobody else to raise us. He looked at my Aunt Fannie, and she said, "No, this is a big house. If you want to leave them here with all of us, keep them all together." She was our second mother.

I was 16 when I left school to get a job at a cigar factory at 701 South Peters in the French Quarters, and I got married when I was 19. We didn't last, but I always spoke to him, yeah. It make the children feel good. I remarried a longshoreman from Lockport, Ernest Colbert. I had a good man with my second husband. He raised my children, and they loved him. When he died, I moved to Tremé to be closer to my work.

I worked at Brennan's as an attendance lady for 35 years. Walking up Royal Street to the restaurant, people in all the little shops say, "Ms. Marion passing. Hey Mom." I said, "Here I am. I'm the Lady in the Powder Room." I kept the bathroom clean and met different people from all over the world. That's educational.

This is still my seat every evening. I'm going to tell you one thing: I'm old enough to drink a Bud Light. And every year I have a birthday party right here, too. Some of my tourist people remember and come around and see me. Strangers stop to talk, I talk. A smile goes a long ways. People like to see that. You frown all the time, you ugly. I tell them, "Don't let the devil get you. Shake him off."

Marion's emphasis on greetings on the street is part of a larger public culture of sociability. Her designation as "Lady in the Powder Room" can be found amongst countless other professions; many had their own greetings. Danny Barker explains:

[T]he ice-cream man, the snoball man, the crab man, each with a song or some noise to identify them and their wares. And about seven in the morning you heard and saw the day peddlers: the charcoal man, cream-cheese man, vegetable man, stone coal man. And night and day people walking along singing jazz songs, sad mournful spirituals. And scores of whistlers: virtuosos whistling jazz songs just like their favorite musicians played their songs. [Barker 2016: 9]

Clarinetist and saxophonist Louis Ford grew up a generation later in the Seventh Ward, where the street songs were still sung:

I can remember hearing the wagon coming down the street. The ice cream man, the vegetable man, the mirliton man. I could be out playing sandlot football with my buddies, and all I'd hear was my mother, "Louis! Louis! Come here! Hurry up! Hurry up!" I got to hurry up and go catch the wagon.

Louis Ford at Preservation Hall on St. Peter's Street in the French Quarter, where he plays regularly. Louis grew up at 2139 Touro Street between North Miro and Galvez in the Seventh Ward. His father, Clarence Ford, played with Fats Domino and his cousin, Charlie Gabriel is one of the most renown clarinet players in the country. Photograph by Bruce Sunpie Barnes.

In the early 2000s, young people in the same neighborhood were no longer raised with the songs of Creole vendors. At John McDonogh Senior High, on the border of the Sixth and Seventh Wards, students lived in homes in the neighborhood that had been passed on through generations. Others came from families who had been sharecroppers on plantations along the Mississippi River before moving to the city. When Sam and Arlet Wylie interviewed their mother, Emelda, for one of the first Neighborhood Story Project books, they learned more about their family connections to St. John the Baptist Parish and the Creole language. Emelda explained:

My grandmother and grandfather were from Wallace, Louisiana, and they spoke Creole when they first came to New Orleans. I remember my grandmother practicing how to speak like people in New Orleans because she had like a French accent when she spoke. Some of the original people still do, but not so much the people that are coming up now. I remember her telling me she worked on trying to lose that. [Wylie and Wylie 2005: 13]

Although many Creole-speaking people tried to assimilate into the dominant Anglo-American culture, Black English in the city is still inflected with Creole vernacular. At John McDonogh, its rhythm filtered through the hallways, and teenagers frequently used Creole words like *repas* (the meal/gathering after a funeral), *bokou* (a lot) and *bankèt* (sidewalk). Other phrases came out as direct translations

Arlet Wylie interviewing her mother, Emelda Wylie, for the Neighborhood Story Project book *Between Piety and Desire*. Many families who first came to New Orleans from Creole-speaking river parishes in Louisiana lived in public housing when it was first built. Emelda grew up in the Desire Public Housing Development before moving to other parts of the Ninth Ward. Photograph by Rachel Breunlin.

from Creole such as "make groceries" (*pour fais marché*). When they asked someone where they lived, they would say, "Where you stay at?" This verb choice comes from the Creole verb *reste*. Derived from the French *rester*, it means both "to stay" and "to live." When the history of these words was incorporated into lessons, they were happy to share more of the poetics of their blended language. They also learned the rules of standardized English grammar much faster. Students who seemed like they weren't paying attention started speaking up more—this time with Creole inflection: "I'm not ignoring you, no."

Reconstructing Creole Through Writing

It has taken a long time for Louisiana Creole to be written as a form of literary expression (see, for example, Clifton 1980). As an act of reclamation, poet and scholar Sybil Kein worked with Ulysses Ricard, Jr., to write in Creole for her book *Gumbo People* (see Kein 1981). In his introduction, Ricard said the collection was the first of its kind, "*un livre ècrit avec le coeur crèole*" (a book written with the Creole heart) (Kein 1981: 1-4).

In 1993, Ricard died when he was only 43 years old. Scholars in Louisiana were understandably devastated when his life's work was cut short. At the time of his death, he was working on the first Creole dictionary using a French orthography developed from fieldwork in Pointe Coupee Parish. He developed curriculum for teaching Louisiana Creole and consulted on many research projects in the region, including transcribing and translating the Records of the Cabildo's trial against San Malo.

In the mid 1990s, Thomas Klinger worked with the Indiana University's Creole Institute and a pan-Caribbean initiative organized by Jean Bernabé at the Université Antilles-Guyane in Fort-de-France, Martinique, to develop *Dictionary of Louisiana Creole* (1998*)*. With linguist Albert Valdman, he began to develop an orthography for Louisiana Creole based on the Haitian standard. In the long road to making Creole an official language, Haiti has moved away from "the influence of the French" to a phonetic alphabet that does not include silent letters. The orthography allows the writing to accurately transcribe the pronunciations of Creole words. Once you learn to read in Creole, you can also speak in Creole.

When this new writing system was introduced in the Caribbean, it provoked a mixed range of emotions. Nobel Prize for Literature recipient, poet Derek Walcott, who spoke English and Creole on his island of St. Lucia, wrote in *What The Twilight Says* about his anger, and sense of loss, at the new orthography:

Creole comes from French. Forced or not, Africans spoke French in slavery, and for the Creole Academy this is an unbearable reality. It demands to have its own writing, and its next step, in its effort to go further and further away from the degradation of slavery and colonialism, would be to invent the hieroglyphics of a new alphabet whose echoes cannot be changed unless every surviving aspect of French is banned....Written Kweyol—why the k for a hard c, for example?—claims an academic and political mandate whose decree I reject because the words are ugly and their sounds cuts off the phonetic subtleties and elegance of the patois...and of course it is this idea of elegance which Creole (Kweyol) orthography condemns as being false or self-deluding French. [Walcott 1998: 228–229]

The question is whether an orthography can capture the nuances of the different variations of spoken language is an issue that every written text will face. In the 15th century, printer William Caxton wrote of his own struggles to render the changes in English as a language after hundreds of years of French being the dominant written language:

> Certaynly it is harde to playse every man by cause of dyversite & chaunge of langage. For in these days every man that is in ony reputacyon in his countre, wyll utter his commynycacyon and maters in suche maners & termes that few men shall understonde theym...therfor...I have reduced & translated this sayd booke in to our englysshe, not ouer rude ne curyous, but in suche termes as shall be understanden, by goddys grace, accordynge to my copye. [Quoted in McCrum, Cran, and MacNeil 1986: 86]

From these first attempts at writing Middle English, the written form of the language began to standardize through consistent use in schools and official uses in government and media.

The same processes have happened for Creole around the world. Moving an oral language into a written one, the spelling is often inconsistent. Lafacadio Hearn wrote about this ongoing issue in the 1800s when he collected Creole proverbs from Louisiana and the Caribbean for his book, *Gombo Zhebes*. Going through transcripts traced back to the 1850s, he pointed out the difficulty in systematizing an oral language without losing nuance. He noted that, "no two authors spell the Creole in the same way," and lamented that *Gombo Zhebes* also spelled many of the same words multiple ways (Hearn 1885: 4)

In Louisiana, where there is no official standardization adopted for Creole, other linguists are working on orthographies that stay closer to the French. In *Kouri-Vini: A Guide to Louisiana Creole Orthography (*Landry, St. Laurent, and Gisclair 2016*)*, some French orthography is maintained in accents and choices of consonants, which is similar to the earlier variations in the Haitian Creole orthography. *Dictionary of Louisiana Creole* moves further away from the French to embrace the phonetic system adopted by the Haitian government. For a French reader, it will take a minute to adjust. However, it does not take long to learn how to read the alphabet as each letter represents a distinct sound.

In Haiti, different spellings of words, especially informal contractions, are still being worked out in print media. The older generation is trying to catch up. As one taxi driver in Port-au-Prince explains:

> When I was in school, all the writing was in French, even though we spoke Creole. I never learned to write in Creole! Then Aristide declared it our official language. I had been out of school for a long time, but I took a class to learn how to write it. At first, we didn't use it too much, but now with WhatsApp, people are writing in it all the time. I didn't want to be left behind.

In *Le Kèr Creole*, we have embraced the pan-Caribbean orthography that extends from WhatsApp users to shopfront signs to the *Dictionary of Louisiana Creole*. In doing so, we recognize we are turning towards the conversations of the pan-Caribbean world more than the francophone literary community, but believe that they are not mutually exclusive. Both directions seek to join local and transnational conversations that are part of all our "quests for relevance" (Thiong'o 1997: 87). With francophone languages including standard French, Haitian, and Louisiana Creole linked together in the 2010 U.S. Census as the fourth most spoken language in the country, all kinds of dialogue seem possible.

We may end here with Chamoiseau's letter at the beginning of *School Days* (1997), where he calls out to all the students of the world whose languages diverge from the languages of power:

> Youngsters,
>
> Of the West Indies, of French Guyana, of New Caledonia, of Reunion, of Mauritius, of Rodriguez, and other Mascerenes, of Corsica, of Brittany, of Normandy, of Alsace, of the Basque country, of Provence, of Africa, of the four corners of the Orient, or all national territories, of all far-flung dominions, of all outlying posts of empires or federations, you have had to face a colonial school, yes, you who in other ways are still confronting one today, and you who will face this challenge tomorrow in some other guide: This voice of bitter laughter at the One and Only—a firmly centered voice challenging all centers, a voice beyond all home countries and peacefully diversal in opposition to the universal—is raised in your name.
>
> In Creole Friendship.

"Pont d'Amour," by Francis X. Pavy. 24"x24" Oil on canvas. Image courtesy of Arthur Roger Gallery.

3.
Creole Friendship:
Music in South Louisiana

Left: The Maple Leaf Bar on Oak Street in the Carrolton neighborhood of New Orleans. Photograph by Bruce Sunpie Barnes.
Right: Leroy Etienne and Bruce Sunpie Barnes in front of La Maison, a music club on Frenchmen Street in New Orleans before a gig in 2018. They have been playing music together for more than 25 years. Photograph by Rachel Breunlin.

In the late 1980s, the Maple Leaf Bar on Oak Street in New Orleans was full of music from all over south Louisiana (Rogers 2008). Close to the Mississippi River in Carrollton, the rambling building with a pressed tin ceiling and red walls always had some light shining from the back where the doors led to a courtyard. There were chess games throughout the day, and poetry readings on Sunday afternoons hosted by Everette Maddox. Tuesday piano nights made famous by Roosevelt Sykes and James Booker continued on with a new generation of professors. Some evenings Bois Sec Ardoin and Canray Fontenot drove over from southwest Louisiana, and Thursday nights John Delafose and the Eunice Playboys took turns with the Filé Cajun Band. Saturday night was Fernest Arceneaux and the Thunders. Bruce Sunpie Barnes was in his early 20s. A harmonica player from the Arkansas delta who had recently moved to New Orleans, he remembers first hearing Fernest and the Thunders:

> They were playing amazingly danceable zydeco, rhythm and blues, la la, boogie-woogie, waltzes, and slow blues. I can remember Fernest singing:
>
> *Take me to the mountaintop,*
> *Love me til my heart stops.*
>
> I was in love with the music of southwest Louisiana.

On the other side of the Atchafalaya Swamp, the region was originally Atakapa-Ishak land. Since the mid 1700s, when it was colonized by the French, it has maintained a strongly francophone culture with many people still speaking Creole and Cajun French. In the 1970s, the region's identity went through a transformation when tourism promotion, funded by the local and state government, marketed 22 parishes in southwest Louisiana as "Acadiana" and "Cajun Country" (Trépanier 1991).

The name upset many people in the Creole community who felt, like the Atakapa-Ishak undoubtedly had before, that their own history and language were being devalued (Spitzer 1986, 2003). Creole activist Takuna El Shabazz openly criticized the renaming for indiscriminately incorporating black Creole cultural expressions into the category of Cajun, and co-founded the Un-Cajun Committee in 1982 to protest the renaming as a "form of white colonialism" (quoted in Mattern 1997: 165, see also Dubois and Melancon 2000: 247). In 1987, other activists created C.R.E.O.L.E. Inc. to promote Creole culture in the region, which they defined as:

> individuals of African descent whose cultural roots have been influenced by other cultures such as French, Spanish, and/or Indian. These individuals have traveled through the centuries carrying their oral history, art forms, culinary skills, religious beliefs and kaleidoscope culture.

El Shabazz criticized the organization on the website Conscientious Council of Black Elders for not discussing systematic violence against black people. The crowds at the Maple Leaf, mostly based in the city, were not as aware of the tensions caused by the cultural and political activism in the southwestern part of the state. Like Sunpie, they came to dance to Fernest and the Thunders' zydeco blues. Sunpie remembers:

> It was a non-stop dancing crowd. I had to push my way to the front. Fernest had long hair he wore in a ponytail with a little tam on his head, and dark glasses in the

Scenes from the Maple Leaf Bar in the late 1980s. ***Left:*** Fernest Arceneaux and the Thunders. ***Middle:*** Bruce Sunpie Barnes watching the dancers at a zydeco show. Photographs courtesy of John Parsons, who owned the Maple Leaf for many years and booked the bands. ***Right:*** The Top Cats: Buckwheat Zydeco, Paul "Lil Buck" Sinegal, and Leroy Etienne. Photograph courtesy of Leroy Etienne.

middle of the night. He was playing a blue accordion, and the band is having a great time.

These integrated crowds would have been unusual for the band to play for in southwest Louisiana. Francis X. Pavy, an artist and musician from Lafayette, remembers going to see Fernest with a few of his friends and being the only white people in the crowd (see also Spitzer 1986: 381):

> We loved their music and clapped at the end of the song. Everyone looked at us. We realized people didn't do that.

Sunpie smiled when he heard this story and explained, "They showed their appreciation more by dancing." Fernest sang in English and Creole. On and off stage, the band joked with each other in a language that most of the audience couldn't understand, and made fun of the way they themselves spoke English when their phrasing came from direct Creole translations. Tony Delafose had a similar experience with the Eunice Playboys:

> I was a musician with my dad and around older people, and I also knew the French language. Even when I wasn't included in their conversation, I still understood what they were talking about. A lot of teasing rather than jokes. It's all about things that happen in life. Some guys can take the teasing, others can't, but we do it all the time. It keeps you family, makes you feel at home—that people care about you who are in the group with you. You'd be surprised how far it goes.

Sunpie began playing rubboard with the Thunders and sat in with the Eunice Playboys. He recalls:

> When I traveled with them, I was learning the history of the area, and feeling the rhythm of the language when they played and talked to each other. I wanted to learn to speak Creole. When the Thunders' drummer, Jockey Etienne, formed the band, the Creole Zydeco Farmers, he invited me to play with them. On the road, they would speak in Creole amongst themselves, but they would switch to English when they spoke directly to me. I protested, "I don't want y'all saying nothing I can't understand!" Their accordion player, Warren Prejean, said, "*Okay. Nou ape pale jus an kreyòl avek twa.*" (*Okay, we are going to speak just in Creole with you.*) I stayed with the Farmers until I started my own band, Sunpie and the Louisiana Sunspots, in 1991. Jockey helped me get started by playing drums whenever he was free.

Jockey also connected Sunpie to his younger brother, Leroy, which led to a musical partnership that has lasted more than 25 years. Leroy played drums with zydeco artists Buckwheat Zydeco and Len August, as well as blues and R&B artists like Solomon Burke and Sherman Robinson. After touring in Europe, he was back in Lafayette. Jockey told him, "I need you to take my place on a gig at the Maple Leaf." Leroy asked what kind of music the Sunspots played and Jockey dismissed it: "Don't worry about that! Just go over there!" This was typical Jockey—generous, with high standards and an insistence that you had to figure some things out by yourself. When we talked about it, Leroy told Sunpie:

> I figured Jockey had talked to everybody about how I was his replacement, so I went over to sit on the drums. You counted off a song, and we began to play.

Hearing Leroy recount his version of the night, Sunpie shook his head, "I didn't know it was you until we took a break! You had Jockey's hat on. Jockey used to wear a little captain's hat." Leroy added:

> I know all his beats, which is why Sunpie didn't catch on right away. But when I played like Jockey, I had to have his blessing.

Brothers

Leroy was just a young boy when Jockey began to play music. His big brother already had one foot out the door. He explains:

> Jockey was 12 years older than me. He was a very excited person who always had ideas he's going to try right away. He was ambitious like our daddy: go, go, go. If he forgets something? "Don't worry, I'll be back."

Left: Clarence "Jockey" Etienne. ***Right:*** Leroy Etienne. Photographs by Bruce Sunpie Barnes.

He's going to take care of what he has to do. If it don't work, well, try it again. He always tried to do what had never been done before just to see if it's going to work. I actually heard him say, "Oh, just play it all wrong, it's gonna come together."

Jockey's point was not to be too shy to get started; through trying you would learn. Before he played music, he learned this lesson when he started racing horses. Jockey explains how he got his nickname:

> I was seven years old when I started riding the horses on the farm. Ran, ran, ran. A white guy come talk to me one day. They had a two-horse race, and did I want to ride? I took a chance with them old quarter horses. Bam! You're finished!

Their father checked Jockey out of school to run races and then brought him back to finish the school day. On the weekends, Leroy came along. He remembers:

> I was small when I used to see them hold the gate before the race. When they let the gate doors go, I used to see Jockey holding on. There was this horse named Caldonia that jumped the fence during a race and threw him in a pond at some distance. He made the sign of the cross and said, "That's it." He got more involved in music after that.

Jockey told us one of the main lessons he learned from racing horses is, "Don't never be the champion. Because the champion, they are always after you." Through straight competition, he realized he preferred collaboration. In his teens, he recorded "with them boys from Crowley." That was J.D. Miller's studio where he was part of sessions with Slim Harpo on "I'm a King Bee" and "Scratch My Back," Lightnin' Slim on "I've Got Love If You Want It," and Guitar Gable on "Congo Mambo." He went on the road with Joe Simon, Johnny Adams, and Solomon Burke.

Music was coming in and out of the Etiennes' house as Jockey went out on the road and then returned home. When we asked him what kind of influence he had on Leroy, Jockey said:

> You got to catch the note. If you can't memorize it, you ain't going to play. I told Leroy, "You better not touch my drums when I'm away because me and mama tight."

Leroy wanted to play drums on his own terms anyway. He learned to be quiet so that he could hear. One of the first rhythms he learned came from his father, who taught him to beat a bamboula rhythm with his hands on the kitchen table. It is a rhythm that has come back to him again and again as he played around south Louisiana, the Caribbean, and Latin America.

Attakapas Poste

Before Leroy was born, his parents, Lawrence and Odelia, raised three daughters and Jockey on the banks of Bayou Queue de Tortue near St. Martinville. When Jockey was young, he said, "*Moun ye sharecrop la ba.*" (People sharecropped over there.) Leroy explains:

> A very old man named Mr. Edgar owned this land near Lafayette and Bayou Tortue. My father worked really hard cutting cane. My mother was a housewife and took care of all the family. She said every time my dad needed help she would get some of her brothers, and they would help him. But when they would go to

the mill to weigh everything to sell it, they never had enough to go around to pay everybody. It was never enough. They never had enough money; they had everything they needed as far as property. They made their whole living out of Bayou Tortue.

Jockey recalls:

> We don't have all the things we have now. At that time, you had to enjoy what you had. It wasn't that bad. No noise. No interference. You grow your own chickens, grow your own pigs. The bayou was there, and that crawfish…man, after the rain! You take your sack and go find big black ones.

Bayou Tortue is said to be named after Chief Celestine La Tortue, a chief of the Atakapa nation. John Swanton, an anthropologist who studied the history of indigenous communities in Louisiana, estimated that in 1698 there were 3,500 Atakapa in the area (Post 1962). In the first half of the 1700s, French colonization in southwest Louisiana was limited, with few settlers crossing the Atchafalaya swamp. When Spain took over Louisiana (1763–1802), the area rapidly changed. Spanish colonial officials considered Louisiana to be on the margins of their prized possessions in Mexico and Peru (Johnson 1992: 46). One of their main concerns was limiting British influence over the entire region, as Britain had gained significant power in North America after winning the French and Indian War (Seven Years War).

In the 1750s, the British had forcibly removed French-speaking Acadians from Nova Scotia. One of the direct accounts of *Le Dérangement* has come from the journals of Abijah Willard, a military captain from Massachusetts who was in charge of executing the orders:

> On August 15, 1755…[a]fter confiscating the Acadians' arms, Willard's men went from house to house, arrested all the Acadian males.…Twelve days later, Willard saw Major Joseph Frye take 200 men to Shepody with orders to "take, burn and destroy all the French in that part of the world." [Grenier 2005: 84–85]

Ten years later, the Spanish colonial government in Louisiana offered Acadian exiles Atakapa and Opelousas land in exchange for acting as a buffer against British settlement in the area. In Canada, the Acadians had been close allies with their Mi'kmaq and Malisset neighbors, and a number of Catholic parishes were home to mixed families. Their loyalty to each other, in fact, had been one of the main reasons they refused to take an oath of allegiance to the British and were forced out (Grenier 2005: 80). In Louisiana, they settled on the banks of bayous, and built their church, St. Martin de Tours, near Bayou Teche in *Poste de Attakapas*, which became St. Martinville.

Bayou Queue de Tortue by Bruce Sunpie Barnes.

Left: D'Jalma Garnier giving a presentation on Creole music at Vermillionville, a living history museum in Lafayette.
Right: St. Martin de Tours Catholic Church in St. Martinville, which was founded by Acadian exiles in 1765. The present church was dedicated in 1844. Photographs by Bruce Sunpie Barnes.

In 2017, master Creole fiddler and ethnomusicologist, D'Jalma Garnier, gave a presentation at Vermillionville, a living history museum in Lafayette dedicated to Cajun, Creole, and Native American people in the region from the arrival of the Acadians through the late 1800s. At the beginning of his talk, he asked a question:

> When the Acadians arrived, there was a Louisiana colony that had already been set up. What they met was a Creole population. Why are we afraid to talk about that?

French colonists in *Poste de Attakapas* developed a cattle industry to supply meat to New Orleans. In the 1776 census of the area, five major cattle ranches, with 50 slaves between them, existed around Atakapa villages (Sluyter 2012:58–59). Jeffery Darensbourg, Alligator band tribal representative of the Atakapa-Ishak and a scholar of indigenous cultures of Louisiana, explains what the early interaction with Acadians would have been like:

> When the Acadians came to this sparsely populated area, native tribes showed them what food to use in cooking. Some are not really eaten so much now, like cat tails or swamp lotus seeds, but others are at the core of what we think of as Cajun and Creole food—shrimp, crawfish, and all the various fish. Cayenne peppers, bell peppers, and squash. Green beans are native. Red beans. And then we have food like okra that comes through Africa.

After the Haitian Revolution, the sugar industry collapsed as Europe and United States refused to recognize the republic as an independent and sovereign country. To pick up the international trade, both white Creole and Acadian families developed plantations in south Louisiana with, generally, more than 50 enslaved people living on each one (Russell 1999: 392). Sugar plantations began to develop along Bayou Teche:

> By the mid-1840s, the lower Teche supported a total of 103 sugarcane planters. Their ranks included 11 Acadians, 50 Frenchmen or French Creoles, and 36 Anglos… the Creole planters resided primarily in St. Martin and St. Mary parishes. [Bernard 2016: 66]

Atakapa land was bought or taken over for these plantations. Jeffery has spent years tracing where the Atakapa-Ishak went after they were forced out of their villages, and found that many families lived near and/or intermarried with Creole people. At the time, they were both labeled "colored." In tracing these legacies, the St. Martin de Tours Catholic Church's records of Atakapa missions help identify families who may have blended into other communities. Jeffery explains:

> In trying to find Atakapa families, you can often go by what Catholic parish they're in; sometimes what Catholic church they attend. In small towns in southwest Louisiana, there are often a white Catholic church and a Black or Creole Catholic church. The latter one usually grew out of a mission to the Atakapa. The towns of Crowley, Carencro, and New Iberia all had mission churches that became churches associated with colored people. If a family is deep enough in those churches, then they're probably connected to the Atakapa-Ishak.

While Cajun French has roots in Brittany, in northwest France, via Canada, for hundreds of years, many families from Acadia lived near black families who spoke Creole (Spitzer 1986: 71). Like white Creole families in the New Orleans region, people with Acadian roots learned this language as well (Trépanier 1991: 164). Around St. Martinville, many older white people explain the way they speak by saying in Creole, "*Mo pale nèg*" (I speak black).

Left: A statue in front of St. Martin de Tours in St. Martinville of an Atakapa-Ishak man with a calumet. Dedicated in 1961, the design is based off a watercolor, "*Desseins de Sauvages de Plusieurs Nations, 1735*" (Sketches of Savages of Various Nations, 1735), by French mason and engineer Alexandre de Batz (1685-1759). The plaque under the statue reads: "Roving savage tribe who settled here prior to the French. Partly Christianized and civilized by missionaries" (see Darensbourg 2016).

Before the colonization of southwest Louisiana, the Ishak, as they traditionally called themselves, or the Atakapa, as they have often been designated by others, were divided into four sovereign bands. The western bands around Lake Charles were known as the "sunset people," and the eastern bands, known as the "sunrise people," lived on the upper Bayou Teche, on lower Vermillion River, near Plaquemine Brule, near Lake Arthur on the Mermentau River, on the Western Great Lake, on Bayou Nezpique, on Bayou Queue de Tortue, and on Lacassine Island. According to *The Historic Indian Tribes of Louisiana*, "[a]round this area, inshore sand ridges, known as *cheniers*, run parallel to the Gulf of Mexico and…create a maze of lagoons, lakes, and active streams…rich in fish, shellfish, bird and animal life, and useful vegetation." Large mounds and middens are also located in the area, including, "a great shell mound, in the shape of an alligator, six hundred feet long" that could be seen on the ridge of Vermillion Parish Great Lake well into the 20th century (Kniffen, Gregory, and Stokes 1987: 47).

Top right: Jeffery Darensbourg, an enrolled member and tribal councilperson representing the Alligator Band of the Atakapa-Ishak Nation, is writing a book about historical representations of the Atakapa, including the statue. *Bottom right:* Artist Alvin "Pem" Broussard at NUNU Arts and Culture Collective in Arnaudville, Louisiana holding one of his rain sticks. Pem traces his family background to both Atakapa-Ishak and Cajun roots. He speaks Louisiana Creole, as well as some Atakapa. Photographs by Bruce Sunpie Barnes.

Top left: Francis X. Pavy holds up a lithophane of Creole accordionist Amédé Ardoin. In the 1930s, Ardoin was viciously attacked after a dance by white men who were angry at the attention he had received from a white woman. Amédé was unable to play music anymore, but his friend, a white fiddler named Dennis McGee, continued to play many of his songs, which an important part of the repertoire of what is considered to be "Cajun" music (Mattern 1997: 161). *Top right:* Zydeco musician Clayton Sampy on his family's land in Carencro, Louisiana. *Bottom:* Sugarcane in southwest Louisiana. Photographs by Bruce Sunpie Barnes.

Interestingly, in Québec, where French has continued to be spoken in Canada, English speakers have been known to taunt *québecois* speakers by saying, "speak white." Michèle Lalonde's poem, "Speak White," connects examples of how people are subjugated by stigmatizing language and color:

> speak white
> tell us again about Freedom and Democracy
> nous savins que liberté est mot noir
> comme la misére est nègre
> et comme le sang se mêle à la poussière des rues d'Alger
> ou de Little Rock
>
> (speak white
> tell us again about Freedom and Democracy
> we know that liberty is a black word
> just as misery is black
> and like the blood that mixes with the dust of the roads
> in Algiers or Little Rock) [Lalonde 1968]

In the poem, Lalonde calls out French colonialism in Algeria and the fight for equal rights in Little Rock, Arkansas, as part of the same struggles for freedom that *québecois* speakers sought in Canada. Anglo-Canadian attempts to suppress it borrowed racist language from the southern United States. We can see how this same social pressure was applied in Louisiana to encourage white speakers of Creole not to identify with black culture as the dominance of Anglo-American culture grew. Under these circumstances:

> The rural whites [felt they] were left with no alternative…but to assume their stigmatized identity, as

Tony Delafose sharing stories about his family's experiences in southwest Louisiana while his son, Jace Delafose, looks on. Photograph by Bruce Sunpie Barnes.

Cajuns, because at least it implied a certain "purity of race." [Waddell 1997: 6]

Yet after the reclamation of the term "Cajun" as a form of whiteness, some older white Louisianans remembered other identities. As one woman from Breaux Bridge explained, *"On s'appelait des Créoles avant cette affaire de Cadjin"* (We were called Creoles before this Cajun business) (quoted in Trépanier 1991: 167). Ironically, Creole musicians of African descent have found themselves marketed nationally this way as well, often being identified as "black Cajuns" (Mattern 1999: 164).

Creole accordionist Clayton Sampy grew up around Carencro, where his family found that many of the power dynamics were related to land. He tells us:

My daddy got his land in 1948. He told me that story *sooo* many times. I was born in 1949 in the new house. Daddy had been looking at this property, and he knew who this property was for, but he knew the Cajun owner wouldn't sell it to him. At that time, that was a no-no: "We don't sell no land to no black people." They don't want you to get ahead.

Daddy knew a white doctor, Dr. Prejean. The doctor said, "What you want me to do?" My daddy said, "You buy it, and afterwards you sell it to me." And you know, my daddy took a chance and gave that man that money? Put the house in his name. And about a month after that, the doctor said, "You ready?" "Yep!" And he got it! Woah! "I'm the man now!!" Oh, yeah, if you had your own property back then, you was a man then. Oh! What?! You had it, bra. That mean that you didn't have to go sharecrop, and rent, and be on somebody else's mercy. You got you your own, yeah. Oh, you was set free.

The Delafose family owned a farm outside of Eunice. Tony Delafose recalls:

Real country. Dirt roads, quiet, peaceful, dusty. They were cotton, rice, and soybean farmers. In their later years, they grew vegetables: beans, okra, cabbage, onion. Growing up, we knew our daddy was sick. I asked him about it later, and I'm glad I did. He said when he was 18 years old, he was working for a burial company and a man pushed him into a grave. He was buried completely. All that was sticking out of the ground was three of his fingers. The guy on the machine saw his fingers, and stopped it. He got a shovel and started digging where he thought my daddy's face would be. And that's what saved him. The pressure of all the dirt being on top of him damaged his heart. Back in the day, people of color really didn't have the power to correct things when they were abused or when there was misconduct. Country living. You can make it if you try.

The quietness of the landscape was more than the open roads; it was also the community silence after acts of racial violence. Many people of color decided to move. The Etiennes followed the migration of other Creole families into the city of Lafayette. When Leroy was nine months old, his father dismantled their house on Bayou Queue de Tortue and brought the cypress lumber to the city. Leroy explains how his father did it:

Top left: Chester Chevalier at his home in Arnaudville. Photograph by Bruce Sunpie Barnes. ***Bottom left:*** St. Catherine's Catholic Church in Arnaudville. Photograph by Rachel Breunlin. ***Bottom right:*** Fernest Arceneaux as a young boy, courtesy of the Arceneaux family.

All nine of his brothers were carpenters, and they helped him rebuild it. When I was growing up, they had more people living in Lafayette who came out of Bayou Tortue, Broussard, New Iberia, Lauraville, Bayou Teche. They were speaking the same style of Creole as my family. The Creole I speak, the pronunciation is on our tongue, not our throat like a lot of French speakers.

One of his neighbors was a *traiteur* (healer) who brought remedies for overwork, heat, and sickness into the city. Leroy recalls:

In the summer, people would get a sensation like a migraine, but worse. They called it *la soley* (the sun). Whether you close your eyes and cut the lights in the room, you swear you are still outside. You would see flashes of light. Eyes hurting you. Your head wanted to explode. It's not something you can take medicine for. I caught it running outside in my bare feet. Ms. Francis sat me in a chair, and wrapped a towel around my head. She took some cold, ice water and started saying prayers while pouring the water over my head. I heard something like water was boiling in a hot pot, and steam started rising. Hot water was coming out, pouring over my face. But I'll tell you what, when she wiped me off, and I got off that chair and went outside, I was good to go. Yeah, I seen a lot of that.

Leroy's family returned to St. Martinville almost every weekend:

> You find a whole army of my family around there. At funerals and weddings, we spoke to our family in Creole. On the weekend, my grandmother would cook and have dinner around a big table. I had two uncles, my mother's brothers Nonc Beloute and Nonc Le Le. They never had kids so they always enjoyed themselves—going on trips and spending a lot of money on their Buicks and Cadillacs. Nonc Beloute showed up for dinner looking like Superfly with gold chains and a shiny black car with all this chrome.

Accompanying family gatherings around the region was an accordion—a small orchestra in a box. After long days of farming around Carencro, Clayton Sampy's and Fernest Arceneaux's fathers played the accordion for their families. Fernest Arceneaux recalls that his father:

> could have been a professional musician, but he was a hard-working man who decided to forego playing to support his large family. You see, there were six brothers and five sisters....My home was really popular back in the 50s because my sister, Mildred, made the finest home-brewed beer in those parts. Clifton [Chenier], [Alton Rubin] Dopsie, and [Hiram] Sampy would come over all the time and sample her beverages and then serenade the neighbors. [Benicewicz 2009]

Tony Delafose shares his family's musical lineages:

> Leo Thomas was my great uncle. He was very popular in his time. When I was about five years old, we went to Elton, Louisiana, for the Fourth of July to listen to his father play the accordion. They had the old-time merry-go-round pulled by a horse. My great-grandfather would sit in the middle and play all day. Talk about fun times.
>
> As I was brought up, many of the famous originators of the French music was right in the same neighborhood. They did the house dances, and they had a couple of old buildings they used for clubs. I would see people like Alphonse "Bois Sec" Ardoin and Marcel Dugas. I used to hang out with my dad and the older guys and they'd do jam sessions. We had an old barn in Swallow, Louisiana, and we used to go every Thursday night to a zydeco jam. All the guys who played the music—Preston Frank, Willis Prudhomme, Leo Thomas—really put something in my soul. The way they played that music from the heart.
>
> The very first instrument I played was a rubboard. We always had one hanging around the house. My dad taught me to play the drums on a cardboard box with two spoons. I was blessed to be talented enough to just be able to pick it up and hear and feel it. So, when my dad would pull his accordion out, I was grabbing the old cardboard box and two spoons. I used my foot on the hardwood floor as a bass drum.

The collaborative music-making young people like Tony experienced is an example of a kind of learning that

A quiet afternoon before Slim's Y-Ki-Ki in Opelousas opens for the evening dance. Photograph by Bruce Sunpie Barnes.

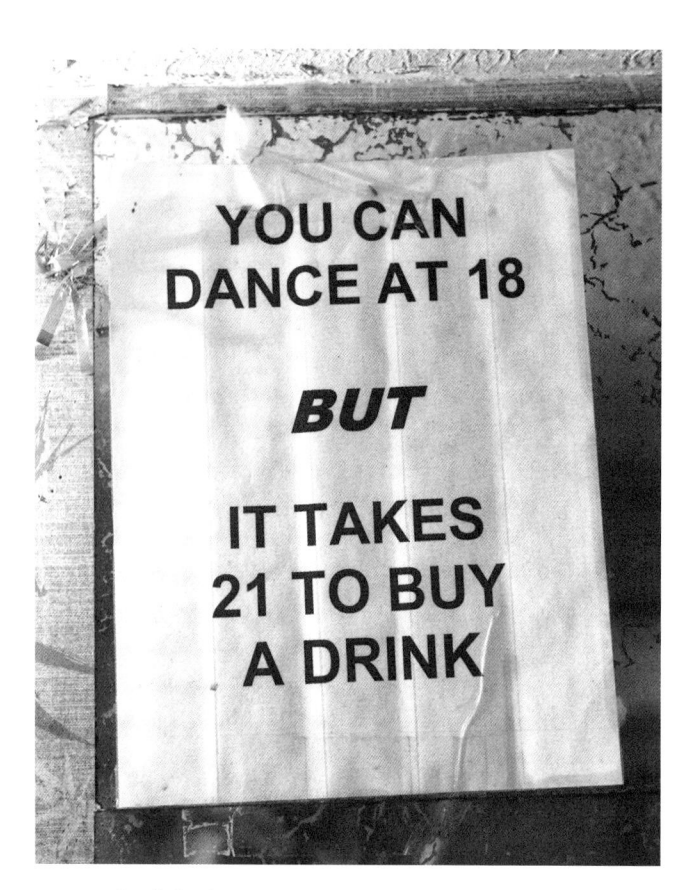

Sign inside of Slim's Y-Ki-Ki in Opelousas. Photograph by Bruce Sunpie Barnes.

ethnomusiciologist Charles Keil says brings out the best of ourselves:

> Collaborative learning, as I understand it, is not a new epistemology but an old ontology, a search for our natural sociability, playfulness, and ability to cooperate. Some may consider it a new support system for prime and genuine culture building, a fresh attack on the inherently isolating and alienating processes of phonetic literacy and linear thinking, but it is also an attempt to recover the oldest forms of humanness that were stolen from our ancestors just a few generations ago....People collaborate best within flexible pre-tested frameworks. [Keil 1992]

In the case of Creole music, the form was given new life with the introduction of R&B from the region. Clifton Chenier and Clayton's uncle, Hiram Sampy, began to transform the culture of the region as they infused Creole music with R&B.

Chester Chevalier grew up sharecropping on the Bushville Plantation outside of Arnaudville. In 1956, Bill Doggett's recording of the instrumental R&B song "Honky Tonk" made it to the *Billboard Hot 100*. Chester explains how the song led him to play music:

> I grew up digging potatoes, picking the cotton, and cutting the sugar cane. My cousin Henry Clay Gordon—we call him Boy Gordon—had a guitar. While he was cutting hair, I was playing with his guitar. A man stopped by and gave him another one. Boy said to me, "You hear this song I'm playing? It's 'Honky Tonk.' Take that guitar home, and when you come back to get your hair cut, I want you to play it." My mom and them would go see Clifton Chenier at the Dauphine Club, and they'd bring me.

Clifton Chenier was born outside of Opelousas in 1925. In his early career, his band opened for Antoine "Fats" Domino (Tisserand 1998:101). He learned Domino's songs and sang them in French and Creole (Olivier and Sandmel 1999: 41). It was an interesting linguistic homecoming. Although Domino was raised in the Lower Ninth Ward of New Orleans and sang in English, he came from a Creole-speaking family in Vacherie in St. James Parish (Coleman 2006: 13). Chenier remembered how much he learned from watching other musicians and was generous on his own gigs. Chester recalls:

> Clifton said, "Put him in a chair by me. He's gonna learn a lot." A bunch of musicians would go there and sit so they could learn. And Clif would tell me, "Just watch the fingers." One day I said, "Let me try myself." That's how I got my rhythm down. I said, "I'm not afraid no more."

Chester knew Fernest Arceneaux from Arnaudville's black Catholic church, St. Catherine's. With Domino's number one singles traveling the world and hit records being produced down the road by J.D. Miller in Crowley, Fernest was inspired to start a rock-n-roll band. He asked Chester if he could help him with some gigs. Chester explains:

> Fernest's daddy came home and asked my daddy if I could play with him because we both was underage. Fernest's daddy said, "I'm all the ways with them kids so you don't have to worry." Our first gig was the church bazaar. Fernest played the guitar until we met Sampy and the Bad Habits. We started following their band. Fernest daddy told Fernest, "You wasting your time. Y'all should play zydeco."

Fernest picked up a triple note accordion and began teaching himself to play. Chester recalls how he learned so many styles by ear:

> Fernest could play zydeco, blues, jazz. Most anything come out, he played. And he said, "Now I gotta sit out there by myself and find the key." In 15, 20 minutes, he'd come back. He had it.

Leroy recalls how the rise of zydeco was supported by the Catholic churches, la las in people's homes, and small clubs around the region:

> In Lafayette, Immaculate Heart of Mary gave the dances and the fairs. The priest would book every big band you could think about: Bobby Bland, Ike and Tina Turner,

Fernest Arceneaux and the Thunders at Richard's Club in Lawtell, Louisiana. Photograph by Rick Olivier.

Little Willie Johnson, Fats Domino, the Platters, Guitar Gabriel. Little Richard came there with the Upsetters. I'll tell you what, they would sell out tickets all the time. At the dances, they would compete for prizes. Most of the time, the trophy giver was the priest. Our oldest sister, Cecile, was a good dancer and won a lot of two-step contests.

Other times people would give parties. Friday night, they parked all the way around the corner in the neighborhoods. And people would start asking, "*Ou se sa?*" (Where is that?) They had big speakers they put on vehicles and would go on the little roads of the neighborhoods announcing, "*Clifton Chenier va joue dan Bon Temps a se swa!*" (Clifton Chenier is going to play in Bon Temps tonight!) Can't even get in!

The Big Apple, Le Bon Temps, the Silver Dollar, the Jazz Room—none of them are there anymore. They broke them down. Get them out of the neighborhood. But back then, boy, they were packed. They stomped the floor to the ground in the Blue Angel. That's not counting the people who stood up on some old soda water cases to look through the windows to see what kind of dance they could pick up on. I was one of those who was peeping in the windows seeing what was going on.

Clayton Sampy returned from the Vietnam War and began playing bass in his family's band, Hiram Sampy and the Bad Habits, but didn't feel connected to zydeco until he heard Clifton Chenier playing the piano accordion at the Blue Angel in Lafayette. He remembers:

> One night I passed by and they had a lot of cars. I had to see what was going on. I couldn't find a parking space, and when I got by the door keeper, I asked, "Who is playing here tonight?"
>
> "Clifton Chenier, the king of zydeco."
>
> I didn't even know they had a king of zydeco! I went inside and got to the bandstand. Clif was young then; Clif was throwing down that night. I couldn't believe what was coming out of that box. I said, "Lord have mercy." He had his crown on with gold teeth smiling and people on the floor just falling out. That night really changed my whole mind about music. That's what I wanted to be, yeah. I got me an accordion.

In 1976, Jockey returned to Louisiana after being on the road with the Blind Boys of Alabama. He said, "Sometimes too much to be married and on the road at the same time." Back home, he was surprised at how zydeco was sweeping through the region. Chester recalls:

> Jockey didn't want to play zydeco; he was still into R&B, but he wasn't making no money. We needed a drummer. We called him. He said, "Well, we off tonight. I'll be there in a little while." He came meet us. When he got through, he said, "If y'all need me, just call." After that, he didn't want to play Rhythm and Blues no more.

It was in the middle of Jockey's transformation that Leroy learned to play the drums. Leroy says:

> When I was young, they used to pass me through the back door of the clubs, make me play the gig, put me back in the car, and make me sleep in the backseat 'til they take me home.

By the time Leroy was in high school, he was traveling with Solomon Burke and playing with zydeco bands around southwest Louisiana.

"I, too, sing America"

In the 1970s and early 80s, Leroy moved to Los Angeles to play music. When he returned home, he joined zydeco bands like Buckwheat Zydeco and Len August. By the early 1990s, Fernest Arceneaux and the Thunders were in the middle of a revival. Their band was touring in Europe, and they were invited to play some gigs on the West Coast. Fernest knew Leroy had lived in California and asked Jockey if he could drive with them. Leroy remembers:

> I went to see Fernest and he asked me, "*Ton frèr koze avek twa pour mennen nouzòt a California? Nouzòt va donn twa an lamen.* (Your brother talk with you? Can you drive us over to California? We going to give you a hand.)
>
> Fernest had an old van. He told the band, "When that guy's driving, you gonna keep it down. We going to drive 55 miles an hour." It took a *long* time. On the way home, a DOT cop stopped us in Arizona. He looked in the van and said, "Where y'all coming from?

I said, "We just came back from playing in California."
"Oh, I thought y'all were some immigrants trying to cross over the border."

Fernest said, "No, we been playing some music."

"Okay. I see you're all speaking English."

Their experience of being mistaken for recent immigrants is not uncommon. As Leroy has traveled with the Sunspots, he has been asked if he is from the Middle East, North Africa, Southern Europe, and Latin America. At a hotel in the northeastern United States, a Russian immigrant working at the front desk thought he was making fun of her accent when he spoke English. Sunpie smoothed the situation over by saying, "English is not his first language, either."

Again and again, the existence of Creole people challenges the racial binary that forces people into categories of "black" and "white." Jeffery Darensbourg explains his own background:

> My birth certificate lists both of my parents as "negro." But whenever someone asked me, "What's your family's ethnicity?" I said things like, "Well, we're kind of a mixture, and I guess we're Creole. We're Black, but we're also French. But then we're also Native American. We're also Spanish." I'm not ashamed of our African ancestry, but it's not at all a complete story. Just as a lot of people want Cajun people to be white, they want Creole people to be black. They want a lot of simple stories.

One of the most well-known examples of the enforcement of a Louisiana law that stipulated that anyone with 1/32nd African ancestry would be defined as black was the 1970 case of Susie Guillory Phipps. Raised as white in a French-speaking family, she learned when she applied for a passport that both of her parents were classified as "colored" on their birth certificates, and thus she would be identified as black. When she asked to change it, the Division of Vital Records traced her genealogy and found that she was 5/32 black, and denied her request (Dominguez 1994). An earlier case from 1849, *Desarzant vs. LeBlanc,* inspired the Creole song "Toucoutou" (Thompson 2001). The exact opposite logic is used by state and the federal governments in documenting Native American descent:

> Can the reader imagine a scenario in which an office of the American government legally compels a person professing anything more than 1/32 Indian blood to accept identification as Indian? No, they are required to show high blood quanta. [Garroutte 2003:43–47]

The fear, of course, is the potential for more land claims. Fernest often said that his family was Indian, and Carencro, where his people are from, is in the heart of Atakapa-Ishak territory. Yet this part of his identity has not been recognized as much as his Creole background. Coming of age during the Civil Rights Movement, he was aware that asserting identities other than black could seem like a betrayal to the community. In the collection of essays, *Confounding the Colorline: The Indian-Black Experience in North America*, Ron Welburn discusses these tensions:

> Privileging Indian heritage creates a breach in Black community stability, cohesion, pride, and unity. Many African Americans feel betrayed by, and sometimes react belligerently toward, anyone they perceive as Black professing to be Indian. In vigorously upholding the one drop of African blood rule, they maintain such persons should be "Black first." Blacks deploy unique cultural mechanism in verbal criticism; the barbed words accompanying chides, ridicule, and haughty ironical put-downs can be emotionally devastating when aimed at those among them they want to "put back in line." [Welburn 2002: 304]

Indigenous scholars and historians of Louisiana emphasize the importance of looking at the time period between the Louisiana Purchase and the Indian Removal Act to understand many tribes' experiences (Verdin 2013, Dardar 2014, Usner 2018). With certain protections in place from the transfer of title from France, the U.S. didn't sign treaties with Indian nations in Louisiana or implement a policy of forced removal. Yet, the federal government's war on Indian nations in the Great Plains and the Southwest must have terrified people who were living here with no protections. Ron Welburn reminds us that as "Indian wars in the West peaked between 1860 and 1890, Indians in eastern communities experienced anxieties about their own survival, anxieties directly proportionate to their hoping to escape detection as Indians in off-reservation communities" (Welburn 2002: 310).

Within this broader context, scholars with connections to Louisiana have been calling for greater attention to mixed Creole/Indian communities (Cranford 2019; Jolivétte 2007). While definitions of Creole often include "Native American" backgrounds, the specific histories and cultural contributions are often vague. A glance at the areas from which zydeco originated in both Louisiana and eastern Texas show a close overlay with traditional Atakapa-Ishak land, yet discussions of zydeco usually do not incorporate considerations of their music (see Lief and Darensbourg 2015 for an exploration of possibilities).

Carolyn M. Dunn and Rain Prud'homme-Cranford's writings are part of a movement to pull these strands back together, often using their own family history to connect Creole identities back to specific tribal people that were impacted by colonialism. Dunn draws on her "Cherokee, Muscogee Creek, Seminole, Cajun, French Creole, and Tunica-Biloxi" background and Cranford shares her identity as "a Louisiana Creole mestiza whose Creole descent includes Choctaw-Biloxi, Ishak, Mvskogean Freedman, and IndoEuropean paternally with Métis (Canada) and Celtic American maternally." Their patchwork poem, "Grandma's Zydeco Stomp Dance" ends with:

Photograph of the family of Villeneuve and Charlotte Fabre, ancestors of Jeffery Darensbourg, taken in New Roads, Louisiana, ca. 1903. Photograph courtesy of Jeffery Darensbourg.

Carry our Grandma's stories
on wide hips laughing
through split lips &
shuffle shake zydeco rhythms.

[Prud'homme-Cranford and Dunn 2017]

The Bounce

What are zydeco rhythms? To the uninitiated, they may seem simple, but as Jockey explains, "There is a bounce in zydeco that's hard for a lot of drummers and dancers to catch. The one, two, three. Continuously." Sunpie explains how it works in dance:

> It is a driving rhythm. As a opposed to lifting your body upward, your hips push down, and the rhythm is caught by bending your knees.

It is this driving rhythm that stomped the floor out of the Blue Angel and was important enough for Fernest Arceneaux and Victor Walker to name one of their albums *Zydeco Stomp* (1981). Sunpie goes on to explain how Jockey taught him more about it while they were playing with Fernest and the Thunders:

> I started playing "Bernadette," which is a fast two-step, and Chester "Toon" Chevalier turned around and told me, "Solo!" It was just Jockey and me on the stage. The rest of the band went to the bar, got a drink, and watched to see what I was going to do. I was feeling good, like I got the rhythm, until Jockey said, "Hey, wait a minute now, who you playing with? Cause you ain't playing with me!" I looked at him and he explained, "You'll kill yourself. You're burning up a lot of energy. Now, you see what you're doing right there? You just play that backwards, and you gonna be with us."

What? Play it backwards? What I learned was Jockey wanted me to fill in the space between the double accents. He led the rhythm by playing a two-beat with his foot on the bass drum and playing the snare with an accented press roll. Part of the bounce in zydeco is really a fast bamboula rhythm. That's Jockey's "1-2-3" push rhythms that gives it the syncopation. It's the same rhythm Leroy learned at their kitchen table from their father. It's in Mardi Gras Indian music as well.

As I spent more time with Jockey, I learned he had an incredible knack for creating a rhythm around any melody that would elevate tunes—make the arrangement stand out. Leroy is great at it, too. You can just sing the song, and he is going to say, "Okay, this is what we're going to do." He's going to show the other instruments what their rhythmic patterns are going to be.

On Fernest and the Thunder's album *Zydeco Blues Party* (1994), the bounce can be heard on "The Fish Song," an old Creole song set to a tango rhythm. The first published mention of "tango" in Louisiana came during the Spanish colonial era. According to historian Kimberly S. Hanger, when Governor Esteban Miró issued the *Bando de Buen Gobierno* (Edict of Good Government) on June 2, 1786, it included an order that prohibited "*los tangos o bailes de negros*" (the tangos, or black dances) be delayed until after prayers ended at St. Louis Cathedral (Hanger: 1997 145). Musicologist Ned Sublette has traced how the tango rhythm has traveled around the hemisphere:

> That four-note habanera/tango rhythm is the signature Antillean beat to this day. It's a single figure that can generate a thousand dances all by itself, depending on what drums, registers, pitches, or rests you assign to which of the notes, what tempo you play it, and how much you polyrhythmic it by laying other, compatible rhythmic figures on top of it. It's the rhythm of the aria Bizet wrote for the cigarette-rolling Carmen to sing (though he lifted the melody from Basque composer Sebastián Tradier), and it's the defining rhythm of *reggaetón*. You can hear it in the contemporary music of Haiti, the Dominican Republic, Jamaica, and Puerto Rico, to say nothing of the nineteenth century Cuban

contradanza. It's Jelly Roll Morton's oft-cited "Spanish tinge," it's the accompaniment figure to W.C. Handy's "St. Louis Blues," and you hear it from brass bands at a second line in New Orleans today. [Sublette 2009: 124]

Fernest said "The Fish Song" was an old folk song that he used to sing in Creole when he was growing up. Sunpie says he was unaware that it had been sung in New Orleans until:

> I was doing research at Tulane's Hogan Jazz Archive in the early '90s. I saw a list of songs that had been reportedly played in Congo Square. In one, "Danse Codan," the lyrics were the same as "The Fish Song"! I later heard Lionel Batiste, Sr., sing it in a club in the Sixth Ward of New Orleans called the Petroleum Lounge. He was on his game singing songs and telling jokes in Creole.

> As I got to know older musicians in both Southwest Lousiana and New Orleans, I learned that saying hello Creole— "*Bonjou, kòmen to ye? Kòmen sa va?*"— would open many doors to conversations about music. I learned the Creole song, "Sali Dam" (Dirty Lady) from jazz musician Placide Adams. His family was from the town of Lafitte, but he lived in the Seventh Ward. When he realized I could catch the double entendres sung in Creole, he taught it to me. It was a gift for taking the time to share his language.

Set on Dauphine Street, "Sali Dam" plays with a casual greeting in French, *salut,* and the Creole word for dirty, *sali,* to tell a story about an encounter with a woman in the French Quarter of New Orleans. These repertoires, infused with a Creole humor, were beginning to slip away in the early 1990s. Louis Ford recognized the same loss:

> I came up at the very tail end with traditional jazz. I was around people like Wallace Davenport, Manny Crusto, Timmy Riley, Big Emory Thompson. I learned from them. They took care of me. I have a book that Manny wrote by hand. He transcribed melodies of all the songs that he had in his repertoire. He wrote everything by hand, and I use that book today.

Other parts of song traditions in New Orleans that were once contained Creole lyrics have been written down without a lot of clarity as to their meaning. The language of Mardi Gras Indian songs is mysterious and contextual, calling on a rhythm that does not exist in English but follows Creole phrasing. For example, in Alan Lomax's *Mr. Jelly Roll*, Alan Lomax writes Jelly Roll Morton's version of "Two Way Pocky Way" with a French orthography:

T'ouwais, bas q'ouwais
Ou tendais
T'ouwais, bas q'ouwais
Ou tendais

A photograph of Fernest Arceneaux that he often used on zydeco dance posters around southwest Louisiana. Image courtesy of the Arceneaux family.

The refrain *Ou tendais* seems to be *Ou tande* (you hear) in Creole. One interpretation of *T'ouwais, bas q'ouwais* could be *Tue, pa kouri* (Kill 'em, don't run), which more metaphorically means "Stand your ground." Sunpie explains that up until the mid 20th century, many Mardi Gras Indians sang in Creole:

> Donald Harrison, Sr., the Big Chief of Guardians of the Flame, and his close friend, Robert Nathaniel Lee from the White Eagles, used to complain that English speakers did not know what the words meant and so the lyrics had moved away from recognizable Creole words. For instance, a common refrain on Carnival day, "Oo na ney," they said, came from *On a le* (We're on our way.).

A "Piano Note" Accordion Teacher

After immersing himself in different styles of music that were connected to the Creole language, Sunpie began to dream of playing an accordion. Throughout Louisiana, there are different varieties, and each creates a distinctive sound. Musicians like Boozoo Chavis and John Delafose played a "button note" accordion with two rows on the right side. This accordion, like other reed instruments such as the harmonica, is tuned to a particular key. If you want to change keys, you must also change accordion. The "triple note" accordion that Fernest played allows for more variation in key and the ability to play blue notes. But the accordion in Sunpie's dream was a piano accordion, affectionately called the "piano note" by musicians

Left: Musician Lionel Batiste, Sr., in the French Quarter of New Orleans in 2012. He grew up in Tremé and knew an extensive repertoire of Creole songs. Photograph by Bruce Sunpie Barnes. *Right:* Placide Adams, one of the great Creole musicians who played New Orleans traditional jazz with Louis Barbarin, Al Hirt and Louis Nelson, as well as blues and R&B with musicians like B.B. King, Ruth Brown, and Chuck Berry. He was also one of the leaders of the Onward Brass Band with Louis Cottrell, Jr. Photograph courtesy of the New Orleans Jazz Museum at the Old U.S. Mint.

who are familiar with the other styles. With a full keyboard on the right side and rows of buttons on the bass side, you can play in any key. Clifton Chenier's style of zydeco emerged from the complexity of the piano accordion.

After years of playing with others, Sunpie turned to seclusion: a time period central to many accordionists in Louisiana. Michael Tisserand writes about it in *The Kingdom of Zydeco*:

> There is a second story-line that bespeaks the power attained by one who learns the accordion…people who tell this tale acknowledge that it came from direct experience. The accordion, many zydeco musicians report, is first learned in secret. They would recall how they would sneak the instrument away from their father, brother, mother, husband. By the time they were caught, they could pull a song. From this Arthurian effort, they were rewarded with the accordion. [Tisserand 1998: 43]

Bois Sec Ardoin, Roy Carrier, and Hiram Sampy all went through this liminal stage. Hiram Sampy's nephew, Clayton, told us about his own rite of passage:

> I didn't want nobody to know I was playing accordion. I stayed in my house for six months. Six months! Every day. Every day as soon as the sun came up until two or three in the morning. I was determined to play the accordion and I was determined to have me a band. If you want something bad enough, you are going to hit it.

> Nobody really taught me. I learned from listening to the old records. It really bring back to my old memory, it make me think about how I lived. Some of the words in the songs have to do with the country. I started getting one piece at a time. And then I got six people rehearsing together. People said, "Y'all ready, yeah." I went to talk to Oscar at Le Bon Temps Roule. It was on Washington Street by the railroad tracks. I had to convince him: "No, I play accordion. I'm telling you, I've got me a band and I'm ready." He booked me, but said, "You know what? You gonna play for the door."

> I was scared the first time. It was the winter time and I was sweating. I wrote down my songs, but I hid them. I was embarrassed to let people see I had written them down. Yes, indeed. When Oscar saw how many people were in there, he said, "I'll give you a price." I said, "No! Give me my door!" And we did good. "Y'all new. Y'all kicking!" Yes, indeed.

Sunpie went through the same process of listening and playing when he began to study the piano accordion:

Clayton Sampy, master teacher of the piano accordion, at his home in Carencro in 2016. Photograph by Bruce Sunpie Barnes.

the right-handed world." I taught myself to play in the mirror. I spent a lot of time in the bathroom. My goal was to have the image in my head of where everything was so I could play by feel without looking down.

I came back to see Clayton and he played for me. He told me, "I am going to show you how to play the whole instrument. A lot of people don't play the whole bass side, but that's where all the rhythm is; where you can command the sound of the instrument. I'm going to teach you how to play both sides and sing in Creole. You will get the whole thing at one time."

Clifton Chenier was the king of this style of accordion, but Clayton Sampy is the king when it comes to teaching how the piano accordion should be played in Creole music. It's obvious if you came out of the Sampy School of Accordion because you know how to play the whole instrument with a full, orchestrated sound. Nathan Williams, the band leader of the Zydeco Cha Chas, named his album *Follow Me Chicken* (1998) as a shout-out to Clayton for showing him how to play. Clayton always told his apprentices, "Follow me chicken, I'm full of corn."

Fernest's nephew, Cory Arceneaux, also learned from Clayton:

If you want to get that thing, you really have to do some shedding. I never did that kind of shedding on the harmonica—it came much easier than that. The accordion has so many things going on: finessing the bellows, pushing and pulling to get the expressive sounds to make it cry and shout in good rhythmic timing. And then you have to learn how to play a melody on top and sing.

Ronald Bob knew I was trying to learn and took me out to Clayton Sampy's place. Samp was very welcoming. "Oh, you from New Orleans? You drove way down in these woods looking for zydeco? I never heard of anyone from New Orleans doing that. Let me see what you got?"

I started to play and he shook his head, "I can't show you nothing."

"What?!"

"I can't show you nothing. You got the accordion upside down. You've got to turn it over." I was devastated. I didn't know there was a right or wrong side to it. Embarrassed, tail tucked between my legs, I almost said, "Forget this." Then I said, "Wait a minute, let me think about it more. I am left-handed. I got to take it to

We lived across the street from my grandparents and Fernest came over to my grandmother's and let me play on his triple-note. We started looking into the accordion and they were expensive. Really, really expensive. My mama said she wasn't buying one because I didn't stick to the guitar. It was in the closet. I found a little red piano note accordion. My budget for Christmas was a 100 dollars and that's how much it was in the Sears catalogue. They bought it for me.

I asked a bunch of people to show me how to play it, but couldn't find a teacher. I knew Clayton Sampy because he used to have these trash trucks and would come by our house to pick up our trash. I saw him playing one time, and Gerard St. Julian said, "Man, you know who you got to show you? Go ask Clayton." The next week he showed up out of the blue at my house and said, "Hey, do you want to go rehearse?" I grabbed my accordion, and he looked at it and said, "No, you ain't going to do nothin with that. It's too small." I had to convince my parents to buy me another accordion! Clayton is the one who taught me all my notes. He'd say, "No, you're working too hard," and showed me easier ways to get to where I was trying to go. Little tricks he taught me, I still play today.

Sunpie explains what he took away from lessons with Clayton:

> I saw how he was keeping rhythm with his foot, how he distributed it through his body, and how he gave himself a good space to sing over the top of it. The fingering positions on the bass side are most important. Leading with the rhythms on the bass side is how you make the chord change. Clayton taught the finger positions to make all the chords the piano note is capable of: one, two, three, six, seventh, flatted sevenths, minors, diminished thirds. The middle finger is on the root note, or tonic note, of whatever key you are playing on. The index finger is on the five chord, and the ring finger is on the sixth. These finger positions allowed me to play one-steps, two-steps, waltzes, *basse bas*, walking bass patterns, shuffles, boogie woogie, rhumbas, and tangos—all the different styles of Afro-Louisiana, the Caribbean, and Africa.

Balanse

On the other side of the zydeco accordion spectrum is the diatonic accordion, which Wilson Anthony "Boozoo" Chavis radicalized in the 1950s. Based outside of Lake Charles, on the edge of the Louisiana-Texas border, Boozoo grew up in a family of sharecroppers. Michael Tisserand wrote of his percussive style of playing:

> [I]f Chenier always reminded his audiences that he came from the country, Chavis makes it plain that he never left…[with his] danceable mix of rural humor, rough blues, and early Creole tunes. [Tisserand 1998: 241]

When Sunpie first started playing the accordion, Chavis was at the height of his comeback, playing fast, danceable songs like "Dance All Night" with English lyrics like, "Take off your wig and throw it in the corner/I can't see why you can't stay a little longer." *Base-ba* waltzes sung in Creole like "Gona la Maison," reminded Sunpie of the waltzes his father, Willie Barnes, Sr., danced to when he was a young boy. Sharing stages with Chavis at concerts in New Orleans and California, he was taken back to his father's stories of Morehouse Parish in the early 1900s. Sunpie shares what his father told him:

> His father, Albert Barnes, was born in 1849 on a plantation in Marion County, Mississippi—the child of the plantation owner and an enslaved woman. His white half-sister brought him to Morehouse Parish when he was three years old. Held in bondage by his own family, he worked in the fields, but was taught to read. My family has spent a long time trying to learn more about how he moved through the world after he was free. He may have continued to move between these families after he married my grandmother, Margaret Moore. My father said he was around half of the time. Growing up, their neighbors called him Teacher. He gave violin and pump organ lessons on the porch.

Top: Bruce Sunpie Barnes playing accordion at the Maple Leaf in the early 1990s. Photograph courtesy of John Parsons.
Bottom: Cory Arceneaux posing with his "piano note" accordion while his uncle, Fernest Arceneaux, holds onto his triple note. Photograph courtesy of the Arceneaux family.

> When he was 11 years old, Albert put my father behind a mule and plow. He remembers Margaret arguing, "That boy too young to use that buster. It gonna ruin his back." When he danced or worked outside, I could see the bow from where the hard work pulled his body down.

Sharecropping into his early 20s, Willie Barnes left the plantation in the middle of the night and moved to Arkansas. He came back numerous times to help other people escape the economic exploitation, and held onto the blues and gospel music from "down home." Sunpie explains:

Left: Willie Barnes, Sr. (*on the right*) at work later in life. *Right*: Bruce Sunpie Barnes with Boozoo Chavis in the mid-1990s. Photographs courtesy of Bruce Sunpie Barnes.

My dad's older brother, Robert, played mandolin and guitar in different blues bands, and my dad taught me to play the harmonica using the tongue blocking method. It reminds me, in some ways, of the shape note singing that came out of the small Baptist churches in Morehouse Parish. It helped me keep good rhythm.

When we would go down home, I loved to hear the way my dad's oldest sister's husband, Sunpie, played barrel house piano. He had lost the tips of his fingers in an accident in a sawmill and shaved his eyebrows for unknown aesthetic reasons. The piano shook the whole house when he played. I used to follow him around like a little duckling. During Easter, my aunts cooked enormous cakes for the Easter Rock celebration, where they arranged the cakes on a table and walked around singing and clapping old songs they took with them from the plantations like, "Rocka My Soul in the Bosom of Abraham." When I first started playing music in college, I remembered my Auntie Fannie calling me "Lil Sunpie" because of my admiration for my uncle. I took the name "Sunpie" to honor my family's musical roots.

Boozoo became one of my main influences, not because we played the same kind of accordion, but because of the way he wrote stories that honored his past while being seriously committed to playing for the dance; for the people. I recognized my family in the music he created out of the land; who found a way to make people look forward to a day up ahead even though their lives were, seemingly, impossibly hard.

The songs create a form of "existential empowerment" that helps us "balance between what is given and what is chosen" (Jackson 1998: 21). In this balance, a person can find power when they experience themselves as subject of their own biographies, when they have agency in their relationships with others. Yet, if western cultures have strived for equilibrium, cultures with a strong West or Central African heritage often have a different goal:

> To "balanse" in Haitian Creole…means to activate or enliven, to dance in a back-and-forth way. To raise energy by playing with conflict and contradiction is to "balanse." Balancing is a way of exposing the true nature of something by bringing it within the forcefield of clashing energies and contradictory impulses. [Brown 1995: 222]

Literary theorist Keith Cartwright used this concept to explore the poetry of Louisiana-born poet Yusef Komunyakaa, and it is also useful in thinking about Boozoo's off-centered rhythms. Boozoo reflected on how he played music:

> Sometimes they say, "Boozoo, you out of time!" My youngest boy, the drummer, he'll say, "Daddy, watch your beat, you jumpin' time," and I tell him, "Don't tell me to watch my beat, you watch me. If it's wrong, do it wrong, with me!" [Olivier and Sandmel 1999: 67–70]

Sunpie was fascinated by Boozoo's sets:

> Boozoo kept his songs short. In a dance hall, he never played a song longer than three minutes. During an

Bruce Sunpie Barnes's grandfather, Albert Barnes, born in 1849. Photograph courtesy of the Barnes family.

hour and a half set, he would often play 40 or 50 songs. Like Fats Domino, the genius of his style in his music was to take you on a journey and have you ride a wave of energy.

Sunpie studied Boozoo's use of energy. Jockey and Leroy, drummers with impeccable, yet unusual, timing, showed him another form of *balanse*: the Creole blues. Whereas the Delta blues is known for its straight 2/4 back-beat, in Louisiana, that beat is held a little longer, creating a slow rocking rhythm like you hear on "*La Ba Che Monroe*." Sunpie first heard the song on *Louisiana Cajun and Creole Music, 1934: The Lomax Recordings* (1987), which is a compilation of songs recorded by John and Alan Lomax for the Library of Congress (see Spitzer 1986, Ancelet 2009). Nick Spitzer makes a connection between the song and the music important to Sunpie's musical upbringing:

> *Jurer*, which means "to testify," was associated especially with the Lenten period in black Catholic communities when instrumental music was restricted. Interestingly, it is not unlike the Easter Rock performance style found in the delta region of north Louisiana…performed in the same period of the year. [Spitzer 1986: 330]

Sunpie's own arrangement of "La Ba Che Monroe" is part of his musical journey combining the Delta blues with Creole accordion music from south Louisiana. When he first started in the early 1990s, he worried what his father would think:

> I had been playing the accordion for about a year before my father saw me with it. He laughed and said, "What you doing with that thang? My daddy played one of those at dances." It was a revelation to me. I thought my dream to play the accordion was taking me farther from my roots, but it was actually bringing me closer. My father asked me, "Well, is you still choking a harp?" I said, "Yeah, I'm going to do both."
>
> "Well, they will like that in Louisiana."

Opposite page: The Neighborhood Story Project's San Malo altar, developed in consultation with Jonathan Scott at the F&F Botanica and Candle Shop, debuted at New Orleans Airlift's Music Box Village's grand opening in November 2016. Sunpie curated a night of music with the Sunspots, OperaCréole, Dédé St. Prix, and Seguenon Kone. In preparation for the event, we created a broadside dedicated to San Malo with Francis X. Pavy and printmaker Kiernan Dunn, which used the image of St. Martin de Porres as a metaphor for St. Marron. We surrounded it with photographs of the swamps where the maroon villages were located. Other offerings included Gwendolyn Midlo Hall's book *Africans in Colonial Louisiana*, the lyrics to "Dirge for San Malo," a time-line of African resistance during the Spanish colonial era created by the Students at the Center Program (2003), auburn cypress leaves, water from the bayous, white shells from the middens, palmetto fans, and purple Louisiana irises. Photograph courtesy of New Orleans Airlift's Music Box Village.

4.
Altars & Invitations

Matt Hampsey, Bruce Sunpie Barnes, Leroy Joseph Etienne, and Michael Harris pour a libation at the Neighborhood Story Project's San Malo altar at New Orleans Airlift's Music Box Village in November of 2016. Photograph courtesy of the Music Box Village.

Altars to the Marvelous

In the 1940s, Robert Tallant wrote *Voodoo in New Orleans*, an often-cited book based on fieldwork from the Works Progress Administration's Federal Writers Project in Louisiana. It is in these pages that we meet Raoul Desfrene, described as a "French Negro," who says he visited the home of Marie Laveau in the late 1880s. On one of her altars, he saw a statue dedicated to Saint Marron, whom he described as:

> a colored saint white people don't know nothing about. Even the priests ain't never heard of him 'cause he's a real hoodoo saint [Tallant 1998 (1946): 78].

Raoul remembered going on Monday nights to a Vodou gathering, called a *parterre*, with Marie Laveau over at Mama Antoine's house on Dumaine Street. In French, *parterre* means "on the ground." In English, it is used to mean a level space in a garden for flowers or the ground floor of a theater auditorium behind the orchestra pit. In Louisiana Creole, it was used to mean a well-organized mélange of different offerings and music. Here is a description of what Desfrene saw:

> A feast was spread for the spirits present on a white tablecloth laid on the floor. The food included congris, apples, oranges, and red peppers. There were lighted candles in the four corners of the room; Raoul recalled their colors as red, blue, green, and brown. A Negro named Zizi played the accordion. [Tallant [1946] 1998: 78]

And then Desfrene shares a beautiful image: women dancing around the *parterre* to the breath of the accordion. They must have known that the spirits love its yearning feeling.

The incorporation of St. Marron into Vodou altars in New Orleans is part of a larger cosmology connected to West Africa. Along the Atlantic coast, the religion has a long history of incorporating new spirits into its pantheon, or creating new ones. As a priest named Fo Idi explained, "We Ewe are not like the Christians, who are created by their gods. We Ewe create our gods, and we create only the gods that we want to possess us, not any others" (Rosenthal 1998: 45). Ewe Vodou practitioners often honor the spirits of enslaved people who were kidnapped in northern Ghana and were either kept as slaves or sold to slave traders crossing the Atlantic ocean. In Togo an American ethnographer, Judy Rosenthal, was informed by an Afa diviner that she should do the same in the United States for the spirits of Africans her ancestors enslaved:

Francis X. Pavy at his studio in Freetown, a neighborhood that was created in Lafayette by freed slaves after the Civil War. Photograph by Bruce Sunpie Barnes.

Why should you not pay your debts to the slave spirits the way we Ewe do? You would be better off for it…. Their spirits are powerful; they can help, heal, and protect you when you need them, if you honor them fully. [Rosenthal 1998: 153]

Creating an altar to connect to difficult and unresolved histories can be, in the words of African art historian Robert Farris Thompson, "a school of being, designed to attract and deepen the powers of inspiration" (Thompson 1993: 147). The ritual practice of tending to the altar— whether it is up for a special occasion or a more long-term commitment—brings about the energy of the ancestors. The hopes of reconciliation and transformation that many people bring to these installations can be seen as part of the project of surrealism proposed by Robin D. G. Kelley in *Freedom Dreams*:

> I traced the Marvelous from the ancient practices of Maroon societies and shamanism back to the future, to the metropoles of Europe, to the blues people of North America, to the colonized and semicolonized world that produced the likes of Aimé and Suzanne Césaire and Wilfredo Lam. The surrealists not only taught me that any serious motion toward freedom must begin in the mind, but they have given us some of the most imaginative, expansive and playful dreams of a new world. [Kelley 2002: 158]

Wildred Lam grew up in the beginning of the 20th century in Cuba with a Chinese father and a mother with a mixed Indian, African, and European background. His work incorporated the cosmology of Santeria and Vodou as well as Carl Jung's theories of archetypes of the collective unconscious. Here is Jung writing on why many artists connect to images of the past that resonate in powerful ways with current times:

> the artist reaches back to the primordial image in the unconscious which is best fitted to compensate the inadequacy of the present. The artist seizes on this image, and in raising it from the deepest unconscious he brings it into relation with conscious elements, thereby transforming it until it can be accepted by the minds of the contemporaries…the spirit of the age is his prompter, and whatever this spirit says is proved true by its effects. [Quoted in van den Berk 2012: 95]

When we began working with Francis X. Pavy for this project, we loved the way he pulled images from his experiences around Lafayette as a musician and artist who crossed the rigid racial boundaries of the area. He explains his own process with art:

> I believe it is one of my gifts or one of my duties to mix the old and the new, and to show elements of cohesion where no association seems possible. I believe I am to mix things, to grasp a fragment of reality to relocate it in other elements of everyday life. Juxtaposition, then, becomes extremely interesting. [Leupin and Pavy 2018: 28]

Similarly, objects on altars are arranged to create juxtapositions that create new references and energy.

As we began to think about creating an altar for San Malo, Sunpie told me about how he first learned about maroon

All Saints Night in Fleming Cemetery in the town of Lafitte in Jefferson Parish, Louisiana. Photograph by Bruce Sunpie Barnes.

settlements. In 1988, Ferdinand Bigard, Big Chief of the Cheyenne Hunters Mardi Gras Indian gang and a community historian, visited him in the Barataria Preserve, and explained the area was one of the places where San Malo's memory was still honored. Soon afterwards, Sunpie visited Fleming Cemetery (see also Spitzer 1986: 190) in the town of Lafitte for All Saints' night. He remembers:

> The graves were illuminated with candles to honor ancestral spirits. After the Cajun families had left the cemetery, Creole and Native Americans came out to give their food offerings. They would leave statues of snakes for Danballah. They also brought palmetto crosses, golden horseshoes, and glass beads for San Malo. I was learning he was like St. Expedite—a spirit you call not just for everyday things but when there is a real emergency; when you need the strongest support in the moment.

The San Malo offerings in Fleming Cemetery join Madeline's song in St. Bernard Parish (1886), the candles on Marie Laveau's altar (1880s), the historical research of Gwendolyn Midlo Hall and Ulysses Ricard, Jr. (1992), and the poetry of Brenda Marie Osbey (1997) to hold onto the power of the maroons (see Voisin 2008). We joined this "changing same" by creating a traveling altar for San Malo and freedom seekers everywhere. In combining the music of *Le Kèr Creole* and the altar, we embraced forms of inquiry that were inspired by what Eva Marie Garroutte calls "Radical Indigenism:"

> It will not suffice to read about or think about such means of inquiry; one must trust them, practice them, live within them. This requires a level of devotion, and perhaps a level of intellectual flexibility.... But those who are willing may learn to understand the world in ways never before available to them. [Garroutte 2003: 108]

We build on and expand Garroutte's concept to include ways of knowing that come from all cultures that still embrace the mystic; that use ceremony for healing and to deepen understandings of our place in the universe (see also Drewal and Drewal 2005; Wilson 2008: 11).

The Power of the Other

To get started on our San Malo altar, we visited the F&F Botanica and Candle Shop, a spiritual supply store on North Broad in New Orleans that had been run by Felix Figueroa for more than 30 years. As Felix had gotten older, his daughter, Tanya, and son-in-law, Jonathan Scott, took care of most of the day-to-day operations of the business. With a degree in comparative religion, Jonathan was interested in the diverse spiritual backgrounds of his customers, knew our ongoing complicated situations in life, and was always willing to help figure out a plan to support our next steps. His advice was grounded in a working knowledge of Catholic saints, Yoruba *orishas*, and other blends of healing practices that New Orleanians shared with him over the years. Each morning, before the day got

Top: Jonathan Scott fulfilling orders at the F&F Botanica and Candle Shop at 801 North Broad Street in New Orleans in 2017. *Bottom:* Statues for sale at the F&F included St. Martin de Porres (*left*), Black Hawk (*middle*), and Chango (*right*). Photographs by Bruce Sunpie Barnes except for Black Hawk, which was taken by Ed Newman at the store in the 1990s.

too busy, he cleared out the energy of the space by burning frankincense. In *Botanicas: Sacred Spaces of Healing and Devotion in Urban America*, Joseph M. Murphy suggests that places like the F&F supported "a creole religion," which he defines as:

> a reconstruction of the grammar and vocabulary of religious symbols from different sources: a structured, meaningful arrangement of elements that communicates in multiple and shifting cultural milieux. [Murphy 2015: 94]

We asked Jonathan if his customers ever looked for a candle or statue to represent maroons. He said that St. Martin de Porres was often used when people wanted to represent a wide variety of people of African descent. From Lima, Peru, St. Martin was the son of a Spanish man and an African or Indian woman from Panama who had been a slave. He is often called the Patron Saint of Interracial Harmony and Social Justice, and his feast day is in the beginning of November. Jonathan explained his popularity:

For a long time, if you had brown skin, and wanted to have a saint who looked like you, St. Martin was the only option for a statue. In the early 1990s, when I first started working at Mr. Felix's shop, people would also come in and buy a St. Anthony or St. Michael statue and paint the faces to match their own.

We didn't have images on candles or prayer cards of African *orishas*. So, for example, Santa Barbara, a white woman, was the saint associated with Shango, a West African *orisha* who is supposed to be a brown-skinned man without his shirt on, wielding an ax. Now it is different. About 10 to 15 years ago, a company in the Dominican Republic began making *orisha* statues. Their largest market is in Brazil, but F&F acts as the distributor for other stores in the Southeast United States.

But in all the years I've been working here, I don't see a lot of loyalty to particular saints and *orishas*. People

The San Malo altar at the Old U.S. Mint was on display in February 2017 for Black History Month. It was a collaboration with the New Orleans National Historical Park and the New Orleans Jazz Museum. Photograph by Bruce Sunpie Barnes.

use what works. If they see it has power, they will try it. Now there is a desire to have something look like you, and there is a desire for otherness. Both have power.

As Jonathan shared his experiences, I remembered something I heard when I first started studying anthropology: it is the pursuit of the self through the other (Taussig 1993).

Colonial Resistance

For many years at the F&F, one of the most popular statues was Black Hawk, the Sauk leader who resisted the Indian Removal Act of 1830 in Illinois (see Jacobs and Kaslow 1991; Berry 1995; Murphy 2015). His story became well-known around the country through his autobiography (Black Hawk 1955 [1833]), and one of the founders of the spiritual church movement in New Orleans, Leafy Anderson, encouraged her congregation to honor him as a spirit with altars and ceremonies (Weymeyer 2000). In 1998, *The Chicago Tribune* reported that there were over 100 spiritual churches in New Orleans, and shared a sermon given by Bishop Oliver Coleman at the Israelite Universal Divine Spiritual Church:

> "Why is it that a Native American . . . is so special to African-American people?" Oliver Coleman begins. "Well, the Indians was oppressed, they was mistreated," he explains, voice rising as people in the pews cry "Yes!" and "That's right!" and "Go on, now!"
>
> "And here black Americans was brought from their native home and brought here in America, and was mistreated, and that's why I believe we can relate to the struggle Black Hawk went through!"
>
> "All right, now!" call back the believers. [*Chicago Tribune* 1999]

Around the same time as the rise of the spiritual churches, Buffalo Bill's Wild West shows were traveling around the country. Often derided for their commercial voyeurism, they were also sites of cross-tribal creativity and innovation. Tara Browner, an ethnomusiciologist and dancer in the Women's Southern Cloth tradition in pan-Indian pow-wows, explains:

> The most recent dances in the pow-wow repertory are the Fancy styles, which came about as a result of Traditional dancers performing at various Wild West shows. In order to better entertain the audiences, dancers were asked to "fancy it up," meaning to speed up their footwork and add spins not found in traditional forms. The dancers complied, and then took the new style back to their communities upon leaving the show. . .Consequently, a new pan-Indian culture, with regional music and dance layered upon a Plains Indian framework, is shaping much of contemporary urban "Indian" identity. [Browner 2002: 49–50]

Plains Indian regalia has been a similar inspiration for people of African descent in both New Orleans and around the Caribbean (Lipsitz 1988, Roach 1992; Smith 1994, Ehrenreich 2004, Breunlin and Lewis 2009). The elaborate suits made for Carnival day are both pursuits of the power of the Other and attempts at reconciling the past:

Top: Big Chief of the Seventh Ward Warriors, Ronald "Buck" Baham, a few days before Carnival in 2005. He is airing out marabou feathers to frame the beadwork on his suit. The use of the word "suit" rather than "costume" amongst Mardi Gras Indians may come from Creole linguistics. "Suit" in Creole is *kòstum*, which derives from the French word *costume*.

Middle: Donald "Dut" Claude coming to pick up Buck on Carnival morning.

Bottom: Dut playing the tambourine on Annette Street as the Seventh Ward Warriors get ready to parade through the neighborhood. Buck has since retired and passed the tribe on to Dut, who is known as one of the best singers in the tradition. Photographs by Rachel Breunlin.

Left: Big Chief of the Creole Osceola with his son, Clarence "Cheyenne" Dalcour III. The three-tiered Peacock Suit was designed by the Dalcours' neighbor, Albert Brown. When Cheyenne was young, his *paren* (godfather) Albert would ask him to help him choose the colors. From these early lessons, he eventually succeeded Albert as designer. Photograph courtesy of the Dalcour family.
Right: Clarence Dalcour, Big Chief of the Creole Osceola. Photograph by Bruce Sunpie Barnes.

> If the purpose of violence is to extinguish certain people, knowledges, and perspectives, then memory continues to resist that violence. Thus the moral burden of the past in the present includes the refusal to succumb to the world of violence and amnesia; witnessing promotes remembrance and works against death and against the comfort of monologue. [Bird Rose 2004: 30]

Clarence Dalcour, Big Chief of the Creole Osceola, explains why he dedicated his Mardi Gras Indian tribe to Seminole resistance in Florida:

> My family on my dad's side comes from the Creole area in Pointe Coupee Parish. My mom's family is from St. Landry Parish in southwest Louisiana. We grew up in a Creole-speaking part of New Orleans called Voscoville. I heard the language around me. I also heard stories about Indian resistance. Osceola was a Seminole chief. He was with a band of Indians down in the swamps of Florida who lived with Africans.

Osceola, born Billy Powell, was raised in the Muskogee village of Talisi in what is now Elmore County, Alabama. Many Muskogee (Creeks) families owned slaves, and Osceola is said to have come from a mixed Creek woman and a Scottish father. After the massacre at Battle of Horse Shoe Bend, Osceola's mother moved her children, with other Creeks, to Florida where they joined the Seminoles. After the Indian Removal Act, Seminole chiefs resisted displacement, saying:

> If suddenly we tear our hearts from the homes around which they are twined, our heart-strings will snap. [Zinn 1980: 143]

For eight years, Osceola led the resistance against removal. He was captured in 1837 when trying to negotiate with the federal government under a "white flag" of truce. In the years that followed, Seminoles, as well the Cherokee, Creeks, and Choctaw, were forced to leave their land. In 1837, more than 1,000 Creeks were forced to board boats headed up the Mississippi to Arkansas. Hundreds lost their lives in a shipwreck on the river. A few months later, the military held about a hundred "Negro prisoners" captured by Creek warriors during the Second Seminole War at Fort Pike on the mouth of Lake Borgne. Some people had been enslaved by the Seminoles and others had escaped white plantations and were living with the tribe as free people (Usner 2018: 85). Just over 53 years had passed since San Malo's settlement to the southeast of the fort had been raided.

Invitation Part I

As our San Malo altar traveled around the city, we invited guests to leave their own offerings and to add comments to a book of reflections. At our exhibit at the Old U.S. Mint, where the Records of the Cabildo that document the trial of San Malo are located, visitors wrote:

> San Malo and all of the maroons remind me that there is always alternative paths to freedom than those presented by society and the state. San Malo's legacy for me is a call to reinforce and defend our communities! To fight!

> I'm from Sudan where people are oppressed and persecuted. I came to the US seeking freedom, but now Trump has banned my people from coming here. Yes, I've found freedom but I wish more of my people will get to experience that, too.

Jean Saint-Malo, pour la liberté et la justice!

For our next installation, I wanted to return to my own neighborhood, the Seventh Ward, to recognize how much the Creole language has been a part of the community and to share the story of the maroons with Mardi Gras Indians like Big Chief Dalcour, who had been telling the stories of black

The set up: The crowd at Bullet's Sports Bar in the Seventh Ward watches Mardi Gras Indians perform during the "Songs for San Malo" concert. Photograph by Bruce Sunpie Barnes.

and Indian resistance to slavery for a long time. The obvious place to host an event was a corner barroom, Bullet's Sports Bar. The owner, Rollins "Bullet" Garcia, Sr., comes from a Creole-speaking family whose cousin, David Ancar, used to live on my block. The former Big Chief of the Seventh Ward Warriors, Ronald "Buck" Baham, one of my long-time mentors in doing ethnography, lives above the bar. In early March of 2017, Sunpie and I went to see Bullet about letting us host the altar with a night of music with the Sunspots and Mardi Gras Indians from the area. He listened to the plan, and then said, with some confidence, "Go ahead."

We asked Buck to help us pull everyone together for St. Joseph's Eve. In other parts of the country, perhaps it's a regular night, but here in New Orleans, March 18 is the night before the elaborate St. Joseph's altars are built by Sicilian Catholics around the region: churches, barrooms, corner stores, and private homes all host them. They are labors of love that welcome the public to come join them for a viewing and, later, a feast of the offerings at the end of the day (see Orso 1990). For many years, many of the corner stores in black neighborhoods were run by Sicilians who lived in the same buildings. Their generosity on St. Joseph's Night may have led Mardi Gras Indians to dress in their suits one last time to enjoy the feasting. Big Chief Dalcour says:

> As it was told to me by older Indians, we celebrated St. Joseph's Night because it was the last night that Indians wore their suits—some of them burned them after that night. And then they had to start sewing again to make a new suit for the next year.

St. Joseph's Night became so popular that the tradition expanded to include an Indian Ball at the San Jacinto Club in Tremé (Barnes and Breunlin 2014: 38). In honor of this creolized tradition, we hosted our event on St. Joseph's Eve in 2017. Bullet spread the word to his regulars, we invited friends who were Mardi Gras Indians, and we advertised around the city. The altar was set up; the candles were lit.

As Leroy sang in Creole, older men in the audience began to remember different phrases from their childhood and started shouting them out: "*Me wi, mon ami!*" (But yes, my friend!) That night, Dalcour said one phrase in Creole had stayed with him since he was a child. When Mardi Gras Indians gathered on Carnival morning, Donald "Dut" Claude's uncle would tell them before they left the house, "*On e tou ansanm*" (We are all together). At Bullet's, Dalcour and Dut sang with Fred Johnson, Ronald "Buck" Baham, Keith "Brick" Price, and other Mardi Gras Indians while people made offerings to San Malo's altar. For a night, when we danced, we danced for the maroons who made their homes on the shell middens of ancient Indians. We danced to bring different parts of Louisiana back together.

Top: Clarence Dalcour and Fred Johnson sing at Bullet's Sports Bar for our event "Songs for San Malo" while Ronald Dumas looks on.
Bottom: The Neighborhood Story Project's San Malo altar at Bullet's. Photographs by Bruce Sunpie Barnes.

The Northside Skull and Bone Gang by Charles Frèger, a portrait photographer who has most recently been working in former maroon communities in South America.

Joe's Cozy Corner on Ursulines and North Robertson in 2004. Photograph by Michel Varisco.

Skeletons

If Mardi Gras Indians mask as a kind of memory work against colonialism (Bird Rose 2004), Sunpie's carnival group, the Northside Skull and Bone Gang, represents what we all face at some point. When talking about people's connection to the tradition, he jokes about "equal opportunity"— humor inherited from Big Chief Al Morris, a Vietnam War veteran and artist who preserved the tradition for many years before sharing it with Sunpie. While Mardi Gras is usually associated with revelry, the before-dawn ritual of the Northside honors the dead and wakes up the living, encouraging us to embrace the time we have left before "you next" (Wehmeyer 2012). Sunpie says he was first aware of ancestral spirits when he was growing up in Arkansas:

> I was sitting with my grandmother, Louvenia Davis Norris, on her front porch. She had just returned from a trip visiting her family in St. Joseph, Louisiana. I saw a man in the back of her car. I asked her, "Big Mama, who is that man?" She asked me, "You see a man back there? What he look like?" I described him and she started to cry. "That's my uncle Joe; he done come back with me." She explained he had passed many years ago, but when she was a young girl, he had taken care of her after she left home. From an early age, the dreams she had about her grandmother, who came to her with ritual scars on her face from Africa, disturbed her father. He sent her away. Big Mama looked in the car and then back at me, "Old Man, you is a seer and a doer, but you can't tell most people. They won't understand."

The Northside Skull and Bone Gang has been a place Sunpie has been able to honor the dead by carrying their spirits for a day—even when they come heavy with unresolved histories. At the beginning of 2004, he had a dream that the proprietor of Joe's Cozy Corner, a jazz club in Tremé, shot someone outside the bar, and Sunpie wrote a song about it called "Too Late" (2012). On January 18, 2004, a shooting actually took place, and a month later, Sunpie sang the song in front of the bar with his gang. He remembers, "The neighborhood was still in shock."

In the early 1990s, Papa Joe Glasper, Sr., had inherited the corner barroom from Ruth Queen. His family was originally from New Roads, a Creole-speaking community in Pointe Coupee Parish, but he had been raised in the city. As a young child, he masked uptown with Brother Tilman's Golden Arrows before moving to the Third Ward and falling in love with "the number one club in the city": the Jolly Bunch Social and Pleasure Club (Breunlin 2004).

When the musician Anthony "Tuba Fats" Lacen passed away, the city hosted his funeral service at Gallier Hall and then a

Left: Fred Johnson, Leroy Etienne, Clarence Delcour, and Donald "Dut" Claude recording "Tro Tar" at the Old U.S. Mint. Photograph by Rachel Breunlin. *Right:* Joseph Glasper, Sr. sitting next to his van parked in front of Joe's Cozy Corner with his favorite stray cat nearby. Photograph courtesy of Rachel Breunlin.

second line of thousands took to the streets, including many, many tuba players. The parade wound its way through the French Quarter and over to Tremé where it disbanded at Joe's. Beer vendors who followed the second line set up nearby. Papa Joe was inside serving drinks, and when he realized someone was trying to do the same thing right next to his bar, he came out and told the man to stop. They argued and witnesses said Richard Gullette, wearing prosthetic legs, hit him. Papa Joe pulled out a gun and fired once into his body, killing him and sending shock waves through the crowd and around the world (Dewan 2004, Reckdahl 2004). Charged with second degree murder, Papa Joe died in Orleans Parish Prison in 2005.

In 2017, Sunpie invited some of the Mardi Gras Indians who hosted "Songs for San Malo" with us at Bullet's to re-record "Too Late" in Creole as "Tro Tar." He believed the tambourines, with the vocal call and response between them, would heat up the song, which is sung in the same timbre as traditional Mardi Gras Indian songs, but with a slightly different accent on the rhythm. Sunpie's lyrics contain some real despair: Your family can no longer help you. You must face what you've done. It's too late; forgiveness is not coming. As we prepared for the performance, I wondered why he had chosen this particular song again—to sing about the end of my friend, and the site of some of my first fieldwork in New Orleans.

In 2004, as Sunpie took to the streets on Carnival morning to sing "Too Late," I was trying to finish writing my first ethnography, a life history of Papa Joe and the role of his barroom in a neighborhood that was quickly gentrifying (Breunlin 2004). Papa Joe had taught me to love traditional jazz; he knew the syncopated beats so well when he danced, he was light on his feet like a much younger man. He taught me about neighborhood connections and emphasized that the ethic of care he brought to his bar was nurtured by the Italian women who helped raise him in the Third Ward. Like them, he enjoyed cooking for everyone and let the barroom become an outpost for all kinds of suppers, club meetings, Indian practices, and fundraisers. Sunday nights were my favorite. Church and parades would end and the bar would slowly fill up with the neighborhood and people from all over the world (see Oldenburg 2001, Breunlin 2004). When I talked to Sunpie about my love of Sundays, he reflected, "They have been more than a day off in this city. They have been a chance for us to define ourselves."

The city has a lightness to it on Sundays that I don't feel other times of the week: it is a day to be oneself, to imagine other possibilities. After the shooting, I struggled to write about any of this. I had never loved someone who had taken another person's life before. I had a hard time getting over what happened. The emptiness on North Robertson and Ursulines still haunts me. Papa Joe died in jail before I had a chance to say goodbye. I didn't see his death as a moral tale. For his funeral, I put together a booklet of some of the oral histories we did together. He had told me:

> Anything you do, you got to love what you do. I love what I do. And I love these young boys coming out here, "Papa Joe, can we practice?" Go on and practice! "Papa Joe, we're gonna barbecue." Go on and do it! You come around here, "Papa Joe, what you got?" I got some

At Joseph Glasper, Sr.'s jazz funeral, his casket was lifted into the crowd and brought into Joe's Cozy Corner to pour a libation. Photograph by Rachel Breunlin.

beans back here. Yeah, you can have some! You got to do something for people. You can't just receive all the time—you got to give back. Come in and go out. Just like breathing—you breathe in, you breathe out.

After the service at St. Augustine Catholic Church, I joined Papa Joe's jazz funeral as it proceeded to Joe's Cozy Corner. The pall bearers took his casket out of the hearse, lifted it through the crowd, and brought him into his barroom one last time. His casket lying on the bar, they poured libations for him. An ancestor. He always wanted to be recognized as an elder; someone who cared for you. My mentor in music and parades had an epic fall from grace, but hundreds of people still joined his second line because of those other acts of care. That's why I was there, too. When I finished his life history a few months later, I offered it up to the universe with a quote from the poet Adrienne Rich: "to the remembering of what they tell us to forget."

Invitation Part II

Nearly ten years after the shooting, Papa Joe began to come back to me as Sunpie and I worked on our book, *Talk That Music Talk: Passing On Brass Band Music in New Orleans the Traditional Way*. At the NSP's workshop in the Seventh Ward, the leader of the Tremé Brass Band, Benny Jones, Sr., traced how Joe's Cozy Corner fit into the lineage of barrooms that supported the development of jazz in the city. In Tremé:

> The neighborhood people would always go to the Caldonia. The Olympia and Onward bands started the funerals and parades at the club and the social and pleasure clubs made the bar one of their stops on their second line.…When the city tore down the Caldonia to build Armstrong Park, Mama Ruth decided to get her own club. She opened up Ruth's Cozy Corner…and I grew up next to the barroom. [Barnes and Breunlin 2014: 94]

As I listened to Benny's story, I thought of my younger self perched on a barstool next to the jukebox as young kids danced to Da Entourage's "Bunny Hop" on the sidewalk and Kermit Ruffins and the Barbecue Swingers played Louis Armstrong's "Skokiaan" in the back room. In between, Papa Joe ran conversations from behind the bar. The writer Leon Forrest articulates my own impressions:

> [S]ome of the most suave and sophisticated men I have ever known were waiters and doormen.… I can only think of them as the cultivated working-class aristocracy, especially when one heard them talk about politics, art, racism, religion in the barbershop or watched them on the dance floor, or overheard them rapping to a lady

Benny Jones Sr., the leader of the Tremé Brass Band, in front of the Neighborhood Story Project in the Seventh Ward of New Orleans. Photograph by Bruce Sunpie Barnes.

at the bar…they embossed high style on everything they touched. [Forrest 1994:49]

To this working-class aristocracy, I would add musicians, who lived in the neighborhood, traveled the world, and met up at Joe's before their gigs.

As we recorded "Tro Tar," I realized I didn't want to just document what had been lost anymore when we also still know what is good, and it is still here. We know that corner spaces have been important to the public culture of the city. While barrooms used to be filled with music in Tremé and the Seventh Ward, zoning changes now mostly prohibit it. The Neighborhood Story Project's corner store building on North Miro and Lapeyrouse could perhaps be transformed, once in a while, to honor the dreams we all have on Sunday nights in New Orleans.

Thus began my campaign to record Creole jazz songs at the NSP. I had my first breakthrough when Sunpie said, "I'd have to think about how that could happen." Up to this point, we had just worked on books there. We had no idea what it would sound like as a recording studio, or if anyone would show up if we hosted a concert. We planned the event with Matt Hampsey, interpretive park ranger at the New Orleans Jazz National Historical Park, who was working with us on *Le Kèr Creole*. We hoped to record traditional Creole songs that had been sung by Danny Barker on *Jazz à la Creole*. In his book, *Buddy Bolden and the Last Days of Storyville*, Barker tells the story of the original recordings from 1947:

> A few years back, Albert Nicholas recorded four Creole songs for Circle Records. James P. Johnson, who played piano on the date, after hearing my accompaniment to Nick's clarinet solo, joined in with me perfectly, and laughing, said, "You cats from New Orleans ain't nothing but a bunch of West Indians." [Barker 1998: 94]

To hold on to this feeling, we asked Preservation Hall if they'd like to partner with us on the concert, which allowed Sunpie

Live recording of Creole jazz songs at the Neighborhood Story Project. Photographs by Rachel Breunlin.

and Matt to invite Detroit Brooks (*guitar*), Louis Ford (*clarinet and saxophone*), Joe Lastie (*drums*), Kerry Lewis (*bass*), Ricky Monie (*piano*), and Molly Ducoste *(violin)*, to play on the gig. Sunpie and Matt's background in blues and zydeco transformed the original songs on *Jazz à la Creole* by playing with faster, more driving rhythms. The expanded band added depth to the harmonies, and Joe Lastie's syncopated drumming created an infectious, danceable groove. Louis Ford reflected on the live recording:

> When we first showed up, I'm gonna tell you, I had my doubts. I said, "Wait. What? Where are we?" I wasn't sure if anyone would show up. I was amazed at the crowd. I really loved it.

As we talked about the night, Louis told us a story about his mother's father, Louis Wiltz, who lived with him for many years in the Seventh Ward. In the late 1960s, Louis was given a tape recorder for Christmas:

> I asked my grandfather to sing something for me to record. He sang a song in Creole. I used to hum it all the time, but I didn't know the name of it. I really got into it.

Louis hummed the song to Sunpie, and they went back and forth trying to figure out the lyrics. Something clicked and Sunpie started to sing lines from *"Mo Pa Lenmen Sa,"* one of the songs they had recorded together for *Le Kèr Creole*. Louis pointed at Sunpie and smiled, "That's it!" His grandfather's voice was coming back to him, this time with the lyrics.

> *Mo pa lenmen kite—mo pa lenmen sa.*
> *Ay yi yi, mo pa leme sa.*
>
> I don't like leaving—I don't like that.
> Ay, yi, yi, I don't like that.

Sunpie and the Louisiana Sunspots performing at the opening of Francis X. Pavy's "In the Company of San Malo."
Photograph by Rachel Breunlin.

Since our first live recording, we have continued to open our doors for events that are inspired by the ethnographies that we are working on. In 2017, Francis X. Pavy began working on an exhibit inspired by our work together around San Malo, which has fit into his larger body of work exploring the history and culture of South Louisiana:

> Pavy is "regional," but only in the sense that he participates in a "new region of the world," as Édouard Glissant has put it, an imaginary region where times ancient and new, places distant and close echo each other and fuse together, a region where an incalculable but finite number of details, emblems or icons, each with their singularities, begin to dialogue with the whole world. [Leupin and Pavy 2018: 20]

We celebrated the opening of "In the Company of San Malo" at our workshop with music from the album. With the candles from the altar glowing, we were inspired to think about what we could learn from the way shrines are run:

> As a concentration of energy, a shrine is full of vitality, expanding and contracting over time. The meanings and associated powers of a shrine can change based on anything from the efficacy of the shrine itself to a dream or vision had by the shrine's owner…the changing demands and desires of spirits and practitioners go hand and hand with the shrine's ongoing synergy of abundance and atrophy. When something "works," more will be added. When something doesn't, a new solution—through divination, prayers, and offerings—will be explored, ad infinitum. [Rush 2013: 33]

Let *Le Kèr Creole* be an offering to the future. Let the music be hummed, tapped out on kitchen tables, and danced to, settling into your spirit to come back to you when you need it. Let the songs be sung in Creole, returning to families whose ancestors spoke the language, and to others who care about this place. And let corners around the world continue to be cosmopolitan crossroads that call us back together.

Francis X. Pavy's "Laman Marron." Augmented photographic lithophane in carved acrylic. Image courtesy of Arthur Roger Gallery.

5.

Creole Song Lyrics

&

English Translations

Hey Nom | Hey Man

Lyrics, Composition, and Arrangement by Leroy Joseph Etienne

Leroy Etienne (*Lead Vocals and Drums*), Bruce Sunpie Barnes (*Accordion*),
Matt Hampsey (*Guitar*), Michael Harris (*Bass*)

Bonjou. Mo pe chante pour mon padna. Mo di li pour leve, epi kouri fe larjen an lòt bord la vilaj. Epi achte kékchoz bon pour li la; pour sa la vi.

Hello. I am singing for my partner. I tell him to get up and go make some money across town. And buy good things for him there, for his life.

Hey nom! [x 4]	Hey man! [x 4]
Gen pour kouri	Got to go
kote louvraj.	where there's work.
Se tan pour kouri	It's time to go
an louvraj.	to work.
Tan pour leve! [x 2]	Time to get up! [x 2]
Hey nom! [x 2]	Hey man! [x 2]
Gen pour kouri	Got to go
dan vilaj.	in town.
Gen pour achte	Got to buy
kèkchoz dan vilaj.	something in town.
Hey nom! [x 2]	Hey man! [x 2]
Hey, gen mon larjen	Hey, got my money
e mon fom.	and my woman.
Gen pour kouri	Got to go
tou kèk-par.	everywhere.
Hey nom!	Hey man!
Huh.	Huh.
Hey nom!	Hey man!
Se bon.	It good.
Lala lala la	Lala lala la
Gen pour kouri.	Got to go.
Hey nom! [x 2]	Hey man! [x 2]
Lalalala	Lalalala
Lala lala	Lala lala
Hey nom!	Hey man!
Hey, hey nom!	Hey, hey man!
Hey nom.	Hey man.
Lala lala	Lala lala

Hey nom! [x 2]	Hey man! *[x 2]*
Gen pour kouri	Have to go
lwen la ba	way over there
Fe louvraj.	to do work.
Kom si, kom sa.	It's so-so.
Huh,	Huh,
Hey nom! [x 3]	Hey man! *[x 3]*
Allon, allon.	Let's go, let's go.
Hey nom,	Hey man,
mach la ba!	walk over there!
Huh!	Huh!
Mach la ba!	Walk over there!
Hey, hey	Hey, hey,
La la	La la
Hey nom!	Hey man!
Hey, nom…	Hey man…

Furniture store between Bayou Queue de Tortue and St. Martinville. Photograph by Bruce Sunpie Barnes.

Nonc Beloute | Uncle Beloute

Lyrics, Composition, and Arrangement by Leroy Joseph Etienne

Leroy Joseph Etienne (*Lead Vocals and Drums*), Bruce Sunpie Barnes (*Accordion*),
Matt Hampsey (*Guitar*), Michael Harris (*Bass*)

Hey Nonc Beloute! Kòmon sa va? Mo pe chante kèkchoz pour twa aster. Mo rapel lontan pase, to te achte char, ki nwar. Mo rapel sa. Se pour twa. Mo lèm sa, okay?

All right! Sa se bon! All right!

Well, hey Nonc Beloute, to rèste lwen la ba.
Hey Nonc Beloute, to gen an fòm ki pel Cora.
Hey Nonc Beloute! Uh-huh!

Sa se bon!
All right!
O yeah!
O huh!
Yeah boy!
Uh-huh.

Well, hey Nonc Beloute, to rèste lwen la ba.
Hey Nonc Beloute, to gen an fòm ki pel Cora.
Hey Nonc Beloute, to achte un char.
Hey Nonc Beloute, son kouler ète nwar. O!

Hey boy!
Come on!
Sa se bon!
All right!

Hey Uncle Beloute! How's it going? I'm singing something for you now. I recall a long time ago, you bought a black car. I recall that. This is for you. I love that, okay?

All right! That's good! All right!

Well, hey Uncle Beloute, you live way over there.
Hey Uncle Beloute, you have a wife named Cora.
Hey Uncle Beloute! Uh huh!

That's good!
All right!
Oh yeah!
Oh huh!
Yeah boy!
Uh-huh.

Well, hey Uncle Beloute, you live way over there.
Hey Uncle Beloute, you have a wife named Cora.
Hey Uncle Beloute, you bought a car.
Hey Uncle Beloute, the color was black. Oh!

Hey boy!
Come on!
That's good!
All right!

Uh huh!	Uh huh!
All right!	All right!
Yeah!	Yeah!
Well, hey Nonc Beloute, to rèste lwen la ba.	Well, hey Uncle Beloute, you live way over there.
Hey Nonc Beloute, to achte twa un gran char.	Hey Uncle Beloute, you bought you a big car.
Hey Nonc Beloute, to gen an fòm ki pel Cora.	Hey Uncle Beloute, you have a wife named Cora.
Hey Nonc Beloute, to rèste lwen la ba. Whoa!	Hey Uncle Beloute, you live way over there. Whoa!
Come on!	Come on!
Sa se bon!	That's good!
Uh huh!	Uh huh!
Sa se bon!	That's good!
Well, hey Nonc Beloute, to rèste lwen la ba.	Well, hey Uncle Beloute, you live way over there.
Hey Nonc Beloute, to gen fòm ki pel Cora.	Hey Uncle Beloute, you have a wife named Cora.
Hey Nonc Beloute, uh huh, to rèste lwen la ba.	Well, hey Uncle Beloute, you live way over there.
Hey Nonc Beloute, to gen fòm ki pel Cora.	Hey Uncle Beloute, you have a wife named Cora.
Achte twa an char.	Bought you a car
Ki char ki kouri la ba.	That car that ran over there.
Achte twa an char,	Bought you a car,
an char ète nwar.	a car that was black.
Hey Nonc Beloute, to rèste lwen la ba.	Hey Uncle Beloute, you live way over there!
Uh huh, well!	Uh-huh, well!
Well, Nonc Beloute, to rèste lwen la ba	Well, hey Uncle Beloute, you live way over there.
Hey!	Hey!
All right Cora!	All right Cora!
Well!	Well!
Ou twa ye?	Where y'at?
Se lwen, lwen, lwen la ba!	It's far, far, far over there!
Bye-bye Nonc Beloute!	Bye-bye Uncle Beloute!

Artwork on the front of a barroom in
Lafayette, Louisiana. Photograph by
Rachel Breunlin.

Tristes | Sad Times

Lyrics, Composition, and Arrangement by Leroy Joseph Etienne

Leroy Joseph Etienne (*Lead Vocals and Drums*)
Bruce Sunpie Barnes (*Accordion*)
Matt Hampsey (*Guitar*)
Michael Harris (*Bass*)

Tristes.	Sad times.
Tou kèkenn travay.	Everybody works.
Oo-o, tristes.	Ohh-oh, sad times.
Tou kèkenn gen traka.	Everybody has trouble.
Oo-oo, se tristes!	Ohh-ohh, it's sad times.
Tou kèkenn gen traka	Everybody has trouble
pou sonye.	care taking.
O-o, se tristes.	Oh-oh, it's sad times
Tou ken pou sonye ye famiy,	Everybody takes care of their family.
Wo-o, tristes.	Whoa-oh, sad times.
O, se tristes.	Oh, it's sad times.
Tou kèkenn fe louvraj	Everybody works
pou sonye ye piti ye.	to care for their children.
Wo-o, se tristes	Whoa-oh, it's sad times
paske	because
an ye vilaj	in their village
pa avek an gran choz.	not much is going on.
Ooo, se tristes.	Ohh, it's sad times.
Wo-a-a, se tristes!	Whoa-ah-ah, it's sad times!

O, me, cher,	Oh, but, dear,
Wo, m'ape jongle.	Whoa, I am remembering.
Oooo.	Ohhh.
Mon maman e mon papa,	My mama and my papa,
Hey, ye pa la!	Hey, they're not here!

O-o, se tristes.	Oh-oh, it's sad times.
Oo-oo-oo,	Ohh-ohhh-ohhh,
ye gen traka	they have trouble
pou sonye ye piti	taking care of their children.
Tou kèkchoz se tristes.	Everything is sad.

A, se tristes.	Ahh, it's sad times.
Wo-a!	Woa-ah!
Kòm an,	One time,
kòm an fwa,	At one time,
moun ye ape kouri a louvraj	people were going to work
me pa fe aster larjen.	but now they don't make money.
O, se tristes, ka-mèm.	Oh, it's sad times, also.
O, wi!	Oh, yes!

U-huh.	Uh-huh.

Bayou Queue de Tortue, by Bruce Sunpie Barnes.

Mo di sa, mo di sa,
O, se tristes!
O-a, o-a, o, se tristes
O me,
tou kèkenn,
tou kèkenn ape fe pa se larjen.
O-o-o, o-a, se tristes.
A, me
o, la ba, it's St. Martin,
o-o-o, se tristes.
Moun ye leve pour kouri a travay,
ape fe pa astèr larjen.
Se tristes.

Kout mwa.
Tou de moun
pa gen
pase pour fe
gran choz.
Oo, se tristes.
O-o,
o-o-o, wi.
Tristes.
Oo, me sa se vre.

I say that, I say that,
Oh, it's sad times!
Oh-ah, oh-ah, oh, it's sad times
Oh, but
everybody,
everybody isn't making money.
Oh-oh-oh, oh-ah, it's sad times.
Oh, but
oh, over there, it's St. Martinville,
oh-oh-oh, it's sad times.
People get up to go to work,
they aren't making money now.
It's sad times.

Listen to me.
All the people
don't have
a way to make
much.
Ohh, it's sad times.
Oh-oh,
oh-oh-oh, yes.
Sad times.
Ohh, but that is true.

Dancers enter Congo Square Preservation Society's Sunday drum circle in Congo Square. Photograph by Bruce Sunpie Barnes.

Danse Codan | Dance Codan

Traditional Arrangement by Bruce Sunpie Barnes

Bruce Sunpie Barnes (*Lead Vocals and Accordion*)
Leroy Joseph Etienne (*Drums and Background Vocals*)
Matthew Hampsey (*Guitar*)
Michael Harris (*Bass and Background Vocals*)
Eric Lucero (*Trumpet*)

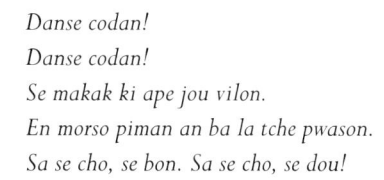

Danse codan!
Danse codan!
Se makak ki ape jou vilon.
En morso piman an ba la tche pwason.
Sa se cho, se bon. Sa se cho, se dou!

Danse codan!
Danse codan!
Me se makak ki ape jou vilon.
En morso piman an ba la tche pwason.
Sa se cho, se bon. Sa se cho, se dou!

Me wi!

[Solo]

Danse codan!
Danse codan!
Me se makak ki ape jou vilon.
En morso piman an ba la tche pwason.
Sa se cho, se bon. Sa se cho, se dou!

Dance codan!
Dance codan!
It's the monkey who is playing the violin.
A little pinch of pepper under the tail of the fish.
It's hot, it's good. It's hot, it's sweet!

Dance codan!
Dance codan!
But it's the monkey who is playing the violin.
A little pinch of pepper under the tail of the fish.
It's hot, it's good. It's hot, it's sweet!

But yes!

[Solo]

Dance codan!
Dance codan!
But it's the monkey who is playing the violin.
A little pinch of pepper under the tail of the fish.
It's hot, it's good. It's hot, it's sweet!

Danse codan!
Danse codan!
Me se makak ki ape jou vilon.
En morso piman an ba la tche pwason.
Sa se cho, se bon. Sa se cho, se dou!

[Solo]

Hey ti la mizèl! Fe makak manje piman!
Se en peu pichoun, se en peu cochon.
Sa se cho, se bon. Sa se cho, se dou!

Hey ti la mizèl! Me, fe makok manje piman.
Sa se cochon. Se en pour ti bon.
Sa se cho, se bon. Sa se cho, se dou!

Dance codan!
Dance codan!
But it's the monkey who is playing the violin.
A little pinch of pepper under the tail of the fish.
It's hot, it's good. It's hot, it's sweet!

[Solo]

Hey little lady! Make the monkey eat the pepper!
It's a bit nasty, it's a bit dirty.
It's hot, it's good. It's hot, it's sweet!

Hey little lady! But make the monkey eat the pepper.
It's dirty. It's a little bit good.
It's hot, it's good. It's hot, it's sweet!

An altar for Shango at Voodoo Authentica in the French Quarter of New Orleans. Photograph by Bruce Sunpie Barnes.

Shango

Lyrics, Composition, and Arrangement by Bruce Sunpie Barnes

Bruce Sunpie Barnes (*Lead Vocals and Accordion*)
Leroy Joseph Etienne (*Drums and Background Vocals*)
Matthew Hampsey (*Banjo*)
Michael Harris (*Bass and Background Vocals*)

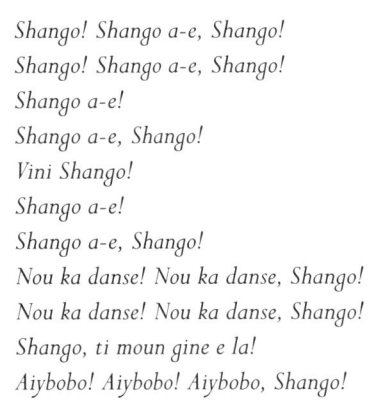

Shango! Shango a-e, Shango!
Shango! Shango a-e, Shango!
Shango a-e!
Shango a-e, Shango!
Vini Shango!
Shango a-e!
Shango a-e, Shango!
Nou ka danse! Nou ka danse, Shango!
Nou ka danse! Nou ka danse, Shango!
Shango, ti moun gine e la!
Aiybobo! Aiybobo! Aiybobo, Shango!

Shango a-e!
Shango, Shango a-e-e!
N'ap tann ou an bariye la, Shango!
A! Shango a-e!
Mmmmmm

Shango a-e!
Shango a-e-e! Shango ah-eh!
Nou ka danse, Shango!
Epi sa cho. Epi sa cho, Shango!
Garde mo, Shango!
Mo ka koze ak ou, Shango!
Dan mo ta lamen, Shango!

Tou moun e la, Shango!
Mo kanpe pou ou, Shango!
Mo pe kanpe pou ou, Shango!
Shango a-e!

Shango! Shango ah-eh, Shango!
Shango! Shango ah-eh, Shango!
Shango ah-eh!
Shango ah-eh, Shango!
Come Shango!
Shango ah-eh!
Shango ah-eh, Shango!
We dance! We dance, Shango!
We dance! We dance, Shango!
Shango, the lil African people are here!
Amen! Amen! Amen, Shango!

Shango ah-eh!
Shango, Shango ah-ehh!
We are waiting for you at the fence, Shango!
Ah! Shango ah-eh!
Mmmmmm

Shango ah-eh!
Shango ah-ehhh! Shango ah-eh!
We dance, Shango!
And that's hot. And that's hot, Shango!
Look at me, Shango!
I talk with you, Shango!
Give me your hand, Shango!

Everybody's here, Shango!
I stand for you, Shango!
I'm standing for you, Shango!
Shango ah-eh!

Shango a-e!	Shango ah-ehh!
Shango a-e, Shango!	Shango ah-eh, Shango!
Shango a-e	Shango ah-ehhhh
Joue, Shango!	Play, Shango!
Joue pou Shango!	Play for Shango!
Danse pou Shango!	Dance for Shango!
Shango a-e! Shango a-e!	Shango ah-eh! Shango ah-eh!
Kòmon tu ye?	How you doing?
Sa ou fe?	How you making it?
Kijan ou ye,	How are you,
Shango?	Shango?
Shango a, Shango a-e!	Shango ah, Shango ah-eh!
Shango a-e! Shango a-e, Shango!	Shango ah-eh! Shango ah-eh, Shango!
Ale, ale, ale, ale Shango!	Let's go, let's go, let's go, let's go, Shango!
Spiri Afrikan,	African spirit,
kouti mo kòm mo pele twa, Shango!	listen to me when I call you, Shango!
Shango.	Shango.
Shango!	Shango!
Vini Shango!	Come Shango!
Kouti mo, Shango!	Listen to me, Shango!
Ti famiy e la, Shango!	Lil family is here, Shango!
Ede mo, Shango! Ede mo, Shango!	Help me, Shango! Help me, Shango!
Me wi, sa cho, Shango!	But yes, that's hot, Shango!
Shango a-eeee!	Shango ah-ehhhh!

Od Pour Odelia | Ode For Odelia

Lyrics, Composition, and Arrangement by Leroy Joseph Etienne

Leroy Joseph Etienne (*Lead Vocals and Drums*), Matthew Hampsey (*Guitar*), Michael Harris (*Bass*)

Kan mo te piti,
lontan pase,
mo maman te achte la banan avek
an nom ki pase
dan lari.
La banan te tou pouri.

Li di, "Hey la ba!"
Nom, li koupe sa cheval, li kouri vi.
Li di, "Hey la ba!"
Li koupe sa cheval, li kouri la.
"Hey la ba!"
Li koupe sa cheval, li kouri vilaj.

Se pa lontan apre sa,
vyeu nom, li mouri la.
Li di, "Hey la ba!"
Nom, li kouri mouri la.
Li vonn la banan tou pouri.
Le banan se tro pouri.

Li di, "Hey la ba!"
Vyeu nom, li kouri la.
Li di, "Hey la ba!"
Li koupe byen cheval.
Li kouri vit la.

When I was small,
a long time ago,
my mama bought bananas from
a man who passed
in the road.
The bananas were all rotten.

She says, "Hey over there!"
Man, he whips his horse, he runs fast.
She says, "Hey over there!"
He whips his horse, he runs.
"Hey over there!"
He whips his horse, he runs to town.

Not long after that,
the old man died.
She said, "Hey over there!"
The man, he was soon dead.
He sold bananas all rotten.
The bananas were too rotten.

She says, "Hey over there!"
The old man, he runs.
She says, "Hey over there!"
He whips his horse good.
He runs fast.

"Hey la ba!"	"Hey over there!"
Vyeu nom, pa lontan, li mouri la.	The old man, not long after, died
Ha la la!	Hey la la!
Hey la ba!	Hey over there!
Kan mo te piti,	When I was small,
mo maman achte	my mama bought
la banan avek vyeu nom.	bananas from an old man.
La banan te tro pouri te ta achte.	The bananas she bought were very rotten.
Nom la kouri dan lari.	The man ran in the road.
Li di, "Hey la ba!"	She says, "Hey over there!"
Vyeu nom kouri dan lari.	Old man runs in the road.
Li di, "Hey la ba!"	She says, "Hey over there!"
Li koupe sa cheval dan lari.	He whips his horse in the road.
Se pa lontan apre sa,	Not long after,
vyeu nom la, li mouri la.	the old man, he died there.
Li di, "Hey la ba!"	She says, "Hey over there!"
Vyeu nom, li mouri la.	The old man, he died there.
Ohhhh, la ba.	Ohhh, over there.

Country road in southwest Louisiana.
Photograph by Bruce Sunpie Barnes.

La Kèkenn Ape Pele Mwa | Someone Keeps Calling Me

Lyrics, Composition, and Arrangement by Leroy Joseph Etienne

Leroy Joseph Etienne (*Lead Vocals and Drums*), Rex Gregory (*Saxophone*),
Matthew Hampsey (*Guitar*), Michael Harris (*Bass*)

La kèkenn	Someone
ape pele mwa,	keeps calling me,
tou le jou	every day
e tou le swa. [x 2]	and every night. [x 2]
Y'ape pele mwa	They're calling me
tou le jou.	every day.
Mo las avek sa.	I'm tired of that.
Mo las avek sa.	I'm tired of that.
Oh, la kèkenn	Oh, someone
ape pele mwa,	is calling me,
tou le jou	every day
e tou le swa.	and every night.
Mo gen pour di li	I got to tell them
pour arèt sa.	to stop that.
Mo gen pour di li	I got to tell them
pour arèt sa!	to stop that!
La kèkenn	Someone
ape pele mwa,	is calling me
tou le jou	every day
e tou le swa.	and every night.
La kèkenn	Someone
ape pele mwa,	keeps calling me,
tou le jou	every day
e tou le swa. [x 2]	and every night. [x 2]
Mo gen pour di li	I have to tell them
por arèt sa.	to stop that.
Mo gen pour di li	I have to tell them
pour arèt sa!	to stop that!
La kèkenn	Someone
ape pele mwa,	keeps calling me,
tou le jou	every day
e tou le swa.	and every night.
Wo!	Whoa!
Ape pele mwa,	Calling me,
tou le jou	every day
e tou le swa.	and every night.

Bonjou Nana | Hello Girl

Lyrics, Composition, Arrangement by Leroy Joseph Etienne

Leroy Joseph Etienne (*Lead Vocals and Drums*), Bruce Sunpie Barnes (*Harmonica*),
Matthew Hampsey (*Guitar*), Michael Harris (*Bass*)

Bonjou nana,
mo konen porkwa to pele mwa.
Wo-o-o, bonjou nana.
Mo konen porkwa to pele mwa.
Mo tande louragan te pase.
O, me, se sa se sa. Huh.

Wo, bonjou nana!
Wo, mo konen porkwa to pele mwa.
Wo-o-o-a-a, bonjou nana!
O, mo konen porkwa to pele mwa.
O, wi.
Mo tande louragan te kase tou kékchoz.
O me, sa se sa.
Wo! Whoaaa, wi!
Bonjou nana!
Wo, mo konen porkwa to pele mwa.

Wo a-a, bonjou nana.
O, mo konen porkwa to pele mwa.
Wo, wi.
Mo konen louragan ki kase tou kékchoz.
O, me, me se sa se sa.
All right. All right!

[Solos]

Wo! Wo! Wo, bonjou nana!
O a, mo konen porkwa to pele mwa.
O, wi.
Wo-a, bonjou nana.
Mo konen, konen porkwa to pele mwa.
O wi.
Mo konen louragan kase tou kékchoz.
Me se sa, se sa!

Wo! Wo!

Bonjou nana.

Hello girl,
I know why you call me.
Whoa oh oh, hello girl.
I know why you call me.
I hear the hurricane passed.
Oh, but that's it. Huh.

Whoa, hello girl!
Whoa, I know why you call me.
Whoa oh oh, ah ahh, hello girl!
Oh, I know why you call me.
Oh, yes.
I hear the hurricane broke everything.
Oh, but that's it.
Whoa! Whoaaa, yes!
Hello girl!
Whoa, I know why you call me.

Whoa ah aah, hello girl.
Oh, I know why you call me.
Whoa, yes.
I know the hurricane that broke everything.
Oh, but, but that's it.
All right. All right!

[Solos]

Whoa! Whoa! Whoa, hello girl!
Oh ah, I know why you call me.
Ohhh, yes.
Whooooah, hello girl.
I know, know why you call me.
Oh, yes.
I know the hurricane broke everything.
But that's it!

Whoaa! Whoaa!

Hello girl.

La Ba Che Monroe | Over by Monroe's

Lyrics, Composition, and Arrangement by Bruce Sunpie Barnes

Bruce Sunpie Barnes (*Lead Vocals and Accordion*), Leroy Joseph Etienne (*Drums and Background Vocals*),
Matthew Hampsey (*Guitar*), Michael Harris (*Bass and Background Vocals*)

Bwa ta kafe, ti fiy,	Drink your coffee, little girl,
bwa ta kafe.	drink your coffee.
Twa, tu mon kite.	You, you leave me.
To tan ale	You gone away
la ba che Monroe.	over by Monroe's.
Kanz jour pase.	Fifteen days pass.
Tu mon kite	You leave me!
Tu tan ale!	You gone away!
Donn mo ta lamen, ti negrès	Give me your hand, little girl.
Mo va di kèkchoz a twa.	I'm going to say something to you.
Mo lenmen pour di kèkchoz	I'd like to say something
kon tu mon fe.	when you did me that.
La ba che Monroe	Over by Monroe's
Ou ta ete?	Where you been?
Tu konen de promis	You know the promise
me tu mon fe?	but you made for me?
Kanz jour pase.	Fifteen days pass.
Mo di, bwa ta kafe	I say, drink your coffee.
Ta mamon e ta papa,	Your mama and your papa,
ye pa lenmen mwa.	they don't like me.

Soley kouche,	The sun sets,
la lun ape leve	the moon is rising.
Kanz jour pase.	Fifteen days pass.
Bwa ta kafe	Drink your coffee
la ba che Monroe.	over by Monroe's.
Tu rès tou la journe.	You stay all day.
Mo di, mo pa konen.	I say, I don't know.
Mo pa konen, che Monroe.	I don't know about Monroe's.
Tu garde mo sur mon jenou.	You see me on my knees.
Mo donn to ma kèr.	I give you my heart.
Tu gen mon kèr, cher,	You have my heart, dear,
me dan ta lamen.	but in your hand.
La ba che Monroe [x 3]	Over by Monroe's *[x 3]*
Twa, tu byen kite.	You, you good and gone.
Woa, mo veu di ma vi	Whoa, I want to say my life
se bato dan louragan.	is like a boat in a hurricane.
Ma vi se kom an bato	My life is like a boat
dan le movetan.	in the storm.
La ba che Monroe	Over by Monroe's
Tu mon kite	You leave me
la ba che Monroe!	over by Monroe's!
Tu mon kite!	You've left me!
Tu mon antre en traka, ti fiy.	You got me in trouble, little girl.
Kanz jour pase	Fifteen days pass.
Bwa ta kafe	Drink your coffee
la ba che Monroe [x 2]	over by Monroe's *[x 2]*
Mo antre,	I'm in,
Mo byen antre en traka, cher.	I really got in trouble, dear.
Tu mo promis.	You promised me.
Twa, tu byen oubliye?	You completely forget?
Mo pa konen. Mo pa konen.	I don't know. I don't know.
Kòfer les nèg kom sa?	Why are people like that?
Kanz jour pase.	Fifteen days pass.
Twa, tu mon kite.	You leave me.
Mo rèst tou sel.	I'm all alone.
Twa, tu kite la ba che Monroe.	You leave, over there by Monroe.
Ta manman e papa,	Your mama and your papa,
ye pa lenmen mwa.	they don't like me.
Mo byen konen.	I know very well.
Tou la journe	All day long
tu kite la ba dan che Monroe	you've gone there, over by Monroe's
La ba che Monroe. [x 6]	Over by Monroe's. *[x 6]*

Opposite page: Sunset on the Mississippi River.
Photograph by Bruce Sunpie Barnes.

Dauphine Street in the French Quarter of New Orleans.
Photograph by Bruce Sunpie Barnes.

Sali Dam | Salty Lady

Traditional
Arrangement by Bruce Sunpie Barnes and the Panorama Brass Band

Bruce Sunpie Barnes (*Lead Vocals and Accordion*) and the Panarama Jazz Band.

Mamzèl Josephine, li rèste sur lari Dauphine.	Ms. Josephine, she lives on Dauphine Street.
Li glise dan an bobin, kase sa ti janm fin	She slips on a spool of thread, breaks her lil skinny leg.
Mo di, "Sali dam, sali dam, sali dam, bonjou."	I say, "Salty lady, salty lady, salty lady, good day."
Sali dam, lese mo wa to gro nwar tou tou.	Salty lady, let me see your big black thing.
Sali dam, sali dam, sali dam, bonjou.	Salty lady, salty lady, salty lady, good day.
Sali dam, lese mo wa to gro nwar tou tou.	Salty lady, let me see your big black thing.
[Solo]	[Solo]
Me si tu kwi an poul pour mo, kwi li dan un frikase.	But if you cook a chicken for me, cook it in a gravy.
Obli pa pour mèt lasòs tomat avek en gro galon diven.	Don't forget to put the tomato sauce with a big gallon of wine.
Mo di, "Sali dam, sali dam, sali dam, bonjou."	I say, "Salty lady, salty lady, salty lady, good day."
Sali dam, lese mo wa to gro nwar tou tou.	Salty lady, let me see your big black thing.
E, sali dam, sali dam, sali dam, bonjou.	Eh, salty lady, salty lady, salty lady, good day.
Sali dam, lese mo wa to gro nwar tou tou!	Salty lady, let me see your big black thing!
[Solo]	[Solo]
E mo di, ti mamzèl Josephine, rèste sur lari Dauphine.	And I say, lil Ms. Josephine, she lives on Dauphine Street.
Li glise dan an bonbin, kase sa ti janm fin.	She slips on a spool of thread, breaks her lil skinny leg.
Mo di, "Sali dam. Salu dam. Sali dam, bonjou."	I say, "Salty lady, hello ma'am. Salty lady, good day."
Salu dam, lese mo wa to gro nwar tou tou.	Hello ma'am, let me see your big black thing.
Sali dam, sali dam, mo di, "Salu dam, bonjou."	Salty lady, salty lady, I say, "Hello, ma'am, good day."
Salu dam, lese mo wa to gro nwar tou tou!	Hello ma'am, let me see your big black thing!

Mo Pa Lenmen Sa | I Don't Like That

Traditional
Arrangement by Bruce Sunpie Barnes

Bruce Sunpie Barnes (*Lead Vocals and Accordion*), Joe Lastie (*Drums and Background Vocals*),
Matt Hampsey (*Guitar*), Detroit Brooks (*Guitar*), Louis Ford (*Tenor Saxophone*),
Kerry Lewis (*Bass*), Ricky Monie (*Piano*)

Mo pa lenmen sa. Mo pa lenmen sa. *Ay, yi, yi, mo pa lenmen sa.* [x 2]	I don't like that. I don't like that. Ay, yi yi, I don't like that. *[x 2]*
Me nom dan lit, fam anba li? *Ay, yi, yi, mo pa lenmen sa.*	But a man in bed, a woman under it? Ay, yi yi, I don't like that.
Mo pa lenmen sa. Mo pa lenmen sa. *Ay, yi, yi, mo pa lenmen sa.*	I don't like that. I don't like that. Ay, yi yi, I don't like that.
Me, fam avek cheuveu kourt? Mo pa lenmen sa. *Ay, yi, yi, mo pa lenmen sa.*	But a woman with short hair? I don't like that. Ay, yi yi, I don't like that.
Mo pa lenmen sa. Mo pa lenmen sa. *Ay, yi, yi, mo pa lenmen sa.*	I don't like that. I don't like that. Ay, yi, yi, I don't like that.
Nom avek gro la bouch? Mo pa lenmen sa. *Ay, yi, yi, mo pa lenmen sa.*	Man with the big mouth? I don't like that. Ay, yi, yi, I don't like that.
Mo pa lenmen sa. Mo pa lenmen sa. *Ay, yi, yi, mo pa lenmen sa.*	I don't like that. I don't like that. Ay, yi, yi, I don't like that.
Fam avek ti janm? Mo pa lenmen sa. *Ay, yi, yi, mo pa lenmen sa.*	A woman with small legs? I don't like that. Ay, yi, yi, I don't like that.
Mo pa lenmen sa. Mo pa lenmen sa. *Ay, yi, yi, mo pa lenmen sa.*	I don't like that. I don't like that. Ay, yi, yi, I don't like that.
[Solos]	*[Solos]*
Oh, me wi, sa cho! Me wi, sa cho la!	Oh, but yes, that's hot! But yes, that's hot there!
[Solos]	*[Solos]*
Mo pa lenmen sa. Mo pa lenmen sa. *Ay, yi, yi, mo pa lenmen sa.* [x 2]	I don't like that. I don't like that. Ay, yi, yi, I don't like that. *[x 2]*
Fam avek cheuveu kourt? Mo pa lenmen sa. *Ay, yi, yi, mo pa lenmen sa.*	But a woman with short hair? I don't like that. Ay, yi, yi, I don't like that.
Mo pa lenmen sa. Mo pa lenmen sa. *Ay, yi, yi, mo pa lenmen sa.*	I don't like that. I don't like that. Ay, yi, yi, I don't like that.
Me, nom dan lit, fam anba li? *Ay, yi, yi, mo pa lenmen sa.*	But, a man in bed, a woman under it? Ay, yi, yi, I don't like that.

Top: Cayetano Hingle and the New Birth Brass Band surprise the audience at the Neighborhood Story Project's Creole Jazz Night.

Bottom: Detroit Brooks, Ricky Monie, Kerry Lewis, Joe Lastie, and Molly Ducoste. Photographs by Rachel Breunlin.

Mo pa lenmen sa. Mo pa lenmen sa.	I don't like that. I don't like that.
Ay, yi, yi, mo pa lenmen sa.	Ay, yi, yi, I don't like that.
Me, nom avek ti jamn? Mo pa lenmen sa.	But a man with small legs? I don't like that.
Ay, yi, yi, mo pa lenmen sa.	Ay, yi, yi, I don't like that.
Mo pa lenmen kite, mo di, mo pa lenmen kite	I don't like leaving, I say, I don't like leaving.
Ay, yi, yi, mo pa lenmen sa.	Ay, yi, yi, I don't like that.
Mo pa lenmen sa. Mo pa lenmen sa.	I don't like that. I don't like that.
Ay, yi, yi, mo pa lenmen sa.	Ay, yi, yi, I don't like that.
Mo fou pa. Mo pa lenmen sa!	I don't give a damn. I don't like that!

Matt Hampsey (*guitar*) and Bruce Sunpie Barnes at the Neighborhood Story Project for the Creole Jazz Night performance. Photograph by Rachel Breunlin.

Creole Blues

Traditional
Arrangement by Bruce Sunpie Barnes

Bruce Sunpie Barnes (*Lead Vocals and Accordion*)
Joe Lastie (*Drums and Background Vocals*)
Matt Hampsey (*Guitar*)
Detroit Brooks (*Guitar*)
Louis Ford (*Tenor Saxophone*)
Kerry Lewis (*Bass*)
Ricky Monie (*Piano*)

Joli fiy, joli fiy, kòfe to pa vyen isi?
Hey, joli fiy, joli fiy, kòfe to pa vyen isi?
Eh, twa konen se mo ki lenmen.
Mo ole twa pour mo, cheri.

Me se kèl joli fiy, la ba dan sa mezon?
Eh, me se kèl joli fiy la, la ba dan sa mezon?
Si tu pa ole mo aster, mo konen byen atan.

Joli fiy, kòfe to pa vyen isi?
Joli fiy, joli fiy, kòfe to pa vyen isi?
Eh, twa konen se mo ki lenmen, nana.
Mo ole twa pour mo, cheri.

Alon joue de blues, cher!

[Solos]

Joli fiy, joli fiy, kòfe to pa vyen isi?
Hey, joli fiy, joli fiy, kòfe to pa vyen isi?

(Twa, to konen byen to gen mo kèr
dan to lamen, cher.)

Eh, twa to konen mo ki lenmen.
Mo ole twa pour mo cheri.

Me se kèl joli fiy, la ba dan sa mezon?
Eh, se kèl ti joli fiy, cher, la ba dan sa mezon.
Si to pa ole mo aster, mo konen byen atan.

Pretty girl, pretty girl, why don't you come here?
Hey, pretty girl, pretty girl, why don't you come here?
Eh, you know it's me who loves you.
I want you for myself, dear.

But who's that pretty girl over there in that house?
Eh, but who's that pretty girl there, over there in that house?
If you don't want me now, I know very well how to wait.

Pretty girl, why don't you come here?
Pretty girl, pretty girl, why don't you come here?
Eh, you know it's me who loves you, girl.
I want you for myself, dear.

Let's play the blues, dear!

[Solos]

Pretty girl, pretty girl, why don't you come here?
Hey, pretty girl, pretty girl, why don't you come here?

(You, you know very well you have my heart
in your hand, dear.)

Eh, you know it's me who loves you.
I want you for myself, dear.

But who's that pretty girl over there in that house?
Eh, who's that pretty lil girl, dear, over there in that house?
If you don't want me now, I know very well how to wait.

Le Zonyon | The Onions

Traditional
Arrangement by Bruce Sunpie Barnes

Bruce Sunpie Barnes (*Lead Vocals and Accordion*), Joe Lastie (*Drums and Background Vocals*), Matt Hampsey (*Guitar*), Detroit Brooks (*Resonator Guitar*), Louis Ford (*Tenor Saxophone*), Kerry Lewis (*Bass*), Ricky Monie (*Piano*), Molly Ducoste (*Violin*)

Le zonyon, le zonyon!	The onions, the onions!
Le zonyon tou de bon marche!	The onions are all good groceries!
Se li isi, se li sa.	This here, that there.
Ma grandmèr tourne li do.	My grandmother twisted her back.
Le zonyon, le zonyon!	The onions, the onions!
Le zonyon tou de bon marche!	The onions are all good groceries!
Se li isi, se li sa.	This here, that there,
Ma grandmèr tourne li do.	My grandmother twisted her back.
Poul kouche?	The hen asleep?
Wi, madam.	Yes, ma'am.
Vou pa monte?	You not lying?
Non, madam.	No, ma'am.
Mo gen bèl calla, tou cho! [x 2]	I have beautiful rice cakes, all hot! *[x 2]*
Bèl calla, bèl calla,	Beautiful rice cakes, beautiful rice cakes,
Mo gen bèl calla, tou cho!	I have beautiful rice cakes, all hot!
Bèl calla tou cho! [x 2]	Beautiful hot rice cakes, all hot! *[x 2]*
Bèl calla, bèl calla,	Beautiful rice cakes, beautiful rice cakes,
Mo gen bèl calla, tou cho!	I have beautiful rice cakes all hot!
[Solos]	*[Solos]*
Le zonyon, le zonyon!	The onions, the onions!
Le zonyon tou de bon marche!	The onions are all good groceries!
Se li isi, se li sa.	This here, that there.
Ma grandmèr tourne li do.	My grandmother twisted her back.
[x 2]	*[x 2]*
Poul kouche?	Hen asleep?
Wi, madam!	Yes, ma'am!
Twa tu pa monte, huh?	You not lying?
Non, madam!	No, ma'am!
Mo gen bèl calla tou cho! [x 2]	I have beautiful rice cakes, all hot! *[x 2]*
Bèl calla, bèl calla,	Beautiful rice cakes, beautiful rice cakes,
Mo gen de bèl calla tou cho!	I have beautiful rice cakes all hot!
Bèl calla tou cho!	Beautiful rice cakes, all hot!
Mo gen bèl calla tou cho!	I have beautiful rice cakes, all hot!
Bèl calla, bèl calla,	Beautiful rice cakes, beautiful rice cakes,
Mo gen bèl calla, tou cho!	I have beautiful rice cakes, all hot!

Tro Tar | Too Late

Lyrics, Composition, and Arrangement
by Bruce Sunpie Barnes

Bruce Sunpie Barnes (*Lead Vocals and Accordion*),
Donald "Dut" Claude (*Tambourine and Vocals*),
Clarence Delcour (*Tambourine and Vocals*),
Leroy Etienne (*Tambourine and Vocals*)
Fred "Malo" Johnson (*Tambourine and Vocals*)

Mama pa ede twa.	Mama can't help you.
[Tro tar]*	*[Too late*]*
Marenn pa edé twa.	Godmother can't help you.
Nenenn pa ede twa.	Godmother can't help you.
Mo di, to sorti la pòrt	I say, you go out the door,
fuzi dan ta men.	gun in your hand.
Tu va mont lez-òt.	You gonna show the others
twa to e gro bet.	you are a big beast
Nenenn pa ede twa.	Godmother can't help you.
Paren pa ede twa.	Godfather can't help you.
Touro pa ede twa.	Touro [Hospital] can't help you.
Dòkte pa ede twa.	Doctor can't help you.
Mo di, mo kouri isi.	I say, I run here.
Mo vini la ba.	I come over there.
Mo na ete	I went
dan karnaval.	in the Carnival.
Mo di, mo gen pa kouròn.	I say, I don't have a crown
Mo pa de moun.	I don't have people.
Me se tro tar.	But it's too late.
Mo chef du skelòt.	I'm the skeleton chief.
Mo sorti la pòrt	I go out the door
dan tra bonnèr.	in the early morning.
Mo di lez-òt,	I say to the others,
"Tu va kouri mouri."	"You gonna die."
"Tu fe tro tar."	"You gonna be too late."
Mo di, se tro tar, cher.	Ah, it's too late, dear.
Aa, se tro tar.	Ah, it's too late.
Nenenn pa ede twa.	Godmother can't help you.
Marenn pa ede twa.	Godmother can't help you.

Top: Fred Johnson, Leroy Etien Clarence Dalcour, annd Donal "Dut" Claude. ***Bottom:*** Bruce Sunpie Barnes. Photographs by Rachel Breunlin.

* In the call and response of the song, "Tro tar" (Too late) is repeated after each line.

112

Paren pa ede twa.	Godfather can't help you.
Touro pa ede twa.	Touro [hospital] can't help you.
Ti neg pa ede twa.	Your little friend can't help you.
Aa, se tro tar.	Ah, it's too late.
Mo di, se tro tar, cher.	I say it's too late, cher.
Se tro tar.	It's too late.
Dan karnaval.	In Carnival,
Wo, Mardi Gra,	Whoa, Mardi Gras
se kouri vit la.	it's coming fast.
du Mardi Gra!	The Mardi Gras!
Endyens vini.	Indians coming!
Endyens kouri la.	Indians running there!
Se traka!	It's trouble!
Fuzi?	Gun?
Li gen kouto	He has a knife
Mo di, se tro tar, cher.	I say, it's too late, dear.
Se tro tar.	It's too late.
Nenenn pa ede twa.	Godmother can't help you.
Marenn pa ede twa.	Mother can't help you.
Papa pa ede twa.	Papa can't help you.
Touro pa ede twa.	Touro [hospital] can't you.
Tu kouri la ba.	You run over there.
Tu reveyèr	You get up
dan asmaten.	in the morning.
Tu peu garde,	You can see
se twa ki mouri la.	it's you who is dead.
Me, se tro tar.	But, it's too late.
Koute skeleton.	Listen to the skeleton.
Le skelòt vini la.	The skeleton comes here.
Mo di, se tro tar.	I say, it's too late.
Dalcour pa ede tar.	Dalcour can't help you.
Dut pa ede tar.	Dut can't help you.
Malo pa ede tar.	Malo can't help you.
Mo di, se tro tar, cher.	I say, it's too late, dear
Me, se tro tar.	But, it's too late
Nenenn pa ede twa.	Godmother can't help you.
Paren pa ede twa.	Godfather can't help you.
Touro pa ede twa.	Touro [hospital] can't help you.
Paren pa ede twa.	Godfather can't help you.
Ohhh, se tro tar.	Oh, it's too late.
Se tro tar.	It's too late.
Ye gen de fuzi la...	They have the gun there...

Works Cited

Accilien, Cècile. 2007. "Haitian Creole in a Transnational Context" in *Just Below South: Intercultural Performance in the Caribbean and the United States*. Edited by Jessica Aders, Michael P. Bibler, and Cècile Accilien. Charlottesville: University of Virginia Press: 76–94.

Alberts, John Bernard. 1998. "Origins of Black Catholic Parishes in the Archdiocese of New Orleans: 1718–1920." Dissertation. Louisiana State University.

Alexander, Charles C. 1965. *The Ku Klux Klan in the Southwest*. Lexington: University of Kentucky Press.

Arceneaux, Fernest, and the Thunders. 1994. "The Fish Song" on *Zydeco Blues Party*. New Orleans: Mardi Gras Records.

Arceneaux, Fernest featuring Victor Walker. 1981. *Zydeco Stomp*. United Kingdom: JSP Records.

Ancelet, Barry Jean. 2009. "Lomax in Louisiana: Trials and Triumphs" on *Folklife in Louisiana: Louisiana's Living Traditions*: http://www.louisianafolklife.org/LT/Articles_Essays/LFMlomax.html. Last accessed February 17, 2019.

———. 2007. "Negotiating the Mainstream: The Creoles and Cajuns in Louisiana." *The French Review* Vol. 80 (6): 1235–1255.

———. 1988. "A Perspective on Teaching the 'Problem Language' in Louisiana." *The French Review* Vol. 61 (3): 345–356.

Ardoin, Alphonse "Bois Sec" with Canray Fontenot. 1974. "'Tit Monde" on *La Musique Creole*. Arhoolie Records.

Barker, Danny. 2016 [1986]. *A Life in Jazz*. Edited by Alyn Shipton with a new introduction by Gwen Thompkins. New Orleans: The Historic New Orleans Collection.

Barker, Danny. 1998. *Buddy Bolden and the Last Days of Storyville*. Edited by Alyn Shipton. London: Cassell.

Barnes, Bruce and Rachel Breunlin. 2014. *Talk That Music Talk: Passing on Brass Band Music in New Orleans the Traditional Way*. New Orleans: The Neighborhood Story Project at the University of New Orleans Press.

Bell, Caryn Cossé. 1997. *Revolution, Romanticism, and the Afro-Creole Protest Tradition in Louisiana, 1718–1868*. Baton Rouge: Louisiana State University Press.

Benicewicz, Larry. 2009. "Remembering Fernest Arceneaux, 1940-2008" in *Blues World*: https://web.archive.org/web/20150811014918/http://bluesworld.com/Fernest.html. Last accessed October 2, 2018.

Bernard, Shane K. 2016. *Teche: A History of Louisiana's Most Famous Bayou*. Jackson: University Press of Mississippi.

Berry, Jason. 1995. *The Spirit of Black Hawk: A Mystery of Africans and Indians*. Jackson: University Press of Mississippi.

Black Hawk. 1955 [1833]. *Black Hawk: An Autobiography*. Edited by Donald Jackson. Champaign: University of Illinois Press.

Blassingame, John W. 1973. *Black New Orleans: 1860–1880*. Chicago: University of Chicago Press.

Bongie, Chris. 1997. "Resisting Memories: The Creole Identities of Lafcadio Hearn and Édouard Glissant." *SubStance* Vol. 26 (3): 153–178.

Breunlin, Rachel. 2004. "Papa Joe Glasper and Joe's Cozy Corner: Downtown Development, Displacement, and the Creation of Community." Masters Thesis at the University of New Orleans.

Breunlin, Rachel and Ronald W. Lewis. 2009. *The House of Dance and Feathers: A Museum by Ronald W. Lewis*. New Orleans: The Neighborhood Story Project at the University of New Orleans Press.

Breunlin, Rachel and Helen A. Regis. 2009. "Can There Be A Critical, Collaborative Ethnography?: Creativity and Activism in the Seventh Ward, New Orleans" in *Collaborative Anthropologies* Vol. 2: 115–146.

Bronner, Simon J. 2005. "Gombo Folkloristics: Lafcadio Hearn's Creolization and Hybridization in the Formative Period of Folklore Studies." *Journal of Folklore Research* Vol. 42 (2): 141–184.

Brosman, Catharine Savage. 2013. *Louisiana Creole Literature: A Historical Study*. Jackson: University Press of Mississippi.

Brown, Becky. 1993. "The Social Consequences of Writing Louisiana French." *Language in Society* Vol. 22 (1): 67–101.

Brown, Karen McCarthy. 1995. "Serving the Spirits: The Ritual Economy of Haitian Vodou" in *The Sacred Arts of Haitian Vodou*. Edited by Donald Cosentino. Los Angeles: University of California Fowler Museum of Cultural History: 205–223.

Brown, William Wells. 1880. *My Southern Home, or The South and Its People*. Boston: A.G. Brown & Co., Publishers.

Brown, Yvonne. 2006. "Tolerance and Bigotry in Southwest Louisiana: The Ku Klux Klan, 1921–23" in *Louisiana History: The Journal of the Louisiana Historical Association* Vol. 47 (2): 153–168.

Browner, Tara. 2002. "Contemporary Native American Pow Wow Dancing" in *I See America Dancing: Selected Readings, 1685–2000*. Edited by Maureen Needham. Urbana: University of Illinois Press.

Cable, George W. 1957 [1880]. *The Grandissimes: A Story of Creole Life*. New York: Hill and Wang, A Division of Farrar, Straus, and Giroux.

———. 1886. "Creole Slave Songs." *Century Magazine* Vol. XXXI (6): 807–828.

Cartwright, Keith. 2005. "Weave a Circle round Him Thrice: Komunyakaa's Hoodoo Balancing Act." *Callaloo* Vol. 28 (3): 850–863.

Chamoiseau, Patrick. 1997. *School Days*. Translated by Linda Coverdale. Lincoln: University of Nebraska Press.

Chicago Tribune. 1998. "The Cult of Black Hawk." Dec 6: https://www.chicagotribune.com/news/ct-xpm-1998-12-06-9812060365-story.html. Last accessed February 4, 2019.

Clark, Emily. 2007. *Masterless Mistresses: The New Orleans Ursulines and the Development of a New World Society: 1727–1834*. Chapel Hill: University of North Carolina Press.

Clifton, Deborah J. 1980. "Voyageur" in *Cris sur le bayou: Naissance d'une poésie acadienne en Louisiane*. Edited by Jean Arceneaux. Montreal: Les Editions Intermède: 77.

Coleman, Rick. 2006. *Blue Monday: Fats Domino and the Lost Dawn of Rock 'N' Roll*. Cambridge, MA: Da Capo Press.

Cosentino, Donald. "Imagine Heaven" in *Sacred Arts of Haitian Vodou*, edited by Donald Cosentino. Los Angeles: UCLA Fowler Museum of Cultural History: 25–53.

Constitution of the State of Louisiana, Adopted in Convention June 18, 1921. Indianapolis: Bobbs-Merrill Company.

Cornelius, Janet Duitsman. 1999. *Slave Missions and the Black Church in the Antebellum South*. Columbia: University of South Carolina Press.

Dardar, T. Mayheart. 2014. *Istrouma: A Houma Manifesto/Manifeste Houma*. Centenary College of Louisiana Press.

Darensbourg, Jeffery. 2016. "Traveling Light." *Situate Magazine*, June 13: www.situatemagazine.com/issue/new-orleans/409/traveling-light. Last accessed September 29, 2018.

Dawdy, Shannon Lee. 2008. *Building the Devil's Empire: French Colonial New Orleans*. Chicago: University of Chicago Press.

———. 2000. "Understanding Cultural Change through the Vernacular: Creolization in Louisiana." *Historical Archaeology* Vol. 34 (3): 107–123.

———. 2000. "Ethnicity in the Urban Landscape: The Archaeology of Creole New Orleans." *Archaeology of Southern Urban Landscapes*. Edited by Amy L. Young. Tuscaloosa: University of Alabama Press: 127–149.

Degraff, Michel. 2005. "'Linguists' Most Dangerous Myth': The Fallacy of Creole Exceptionalism." *Language and Society* Vol. 34 (4): 533–591.

Desdunes, Adolphe Lucien. 1973 [1911]. *Our People and Our History: Fifty Creole Portraits*. Translated and edited by Sister Dorothea Olga McCants, Daughter of the Cross. Baton Rouge: Louisiana State University Press.

Dessens, Nathalie. 2007. *From San Domingue to New Orleans: Migration and Influences*. Gainesville: University Press of Florida.

Devore, Donald E. and Joseph Logdson. 2011. *Crescent City Schools*. Lafayette: University of Louisiana at Lafayette.

Dewan, Shaila. 2004. "Fatal Shooting Prompts Bar's Closing and a Cultural Debate." *The New York Times*, June 17: https://www.nytimes.com/2004/06/17/us/fatal-shooting-prompts-bar-s-closing-and-a-cultural-debate.html. Last accessed on February 5, 2019.

Dominguez, Virginia. 1994. *White by Definition: Social Classification in Creole Louisiana*. New Brunswick: Rutgers.

Drewal, Henry and Margaret Thompson Drewal. 1978. "Senses in Understanding African Art." *African Arts* Vol. 38 (3): 4–5+88.

Dubois, Sylvie and Megan Melancon. 2000. "Creole Is, Creole Ain't: Diachronic and Synchronic Attitudes toward Creole Identity in Southern Louisiana." *Language in Society* Vol. 29 (2): 237–258.

Dunbar-Ortiz, Roxanne. 2014. *An Indigenous Peoples' History of the United States*. Boston: Beacon Press.

Ehrenreich, Jeffrey. 2004. "Bodies, Beads, Bones, and Feathers: The Masking Traditions of Mardi Gras Indians in New Orleans, A Photo Essay." *City & Society* Vol. 16 (1): 117–130.

Estaville, Lawrence E., Jr. 1990. "The Louisiana French Language in the Nineteenth Century." *Southeastern Geographer* Vol. 30 (2): 107–120.

Estes, David C. 2000. "The St. Ann Shrine in New Orleans: Popular Catholicism in Local, National, and International Contexts." *Louisiana Folklore Miscellany* Vol. XV: 51–58.

Evans, Freddi Williams. 2011. *Congo Square: African Roots in New Orleans*. Lafayette: University of Louisiana, Lafayette.

Fairclough, Adam. 1995. *Race and Democracy: The Civil Rights Struggle in Louisiana, 1915–1972*. Athens: University of Georgia Press.

Fandrich, Ina Johanna. 2005. *The Mysterious Voodoo Queen, Marie Laveaux: A Study of Powerful Female Leadership in Nineteenth Century New Orleans*. Abingdon-on-Thames: Routledge.

Faulk, James Donald. 1977. *Cajun French I*. Louisiana: Cajun Press, Inc.

Foner, Eric. 1988. *Reconstruction: America's Unfinished Revolution, 1863–1877*. New York: Perennial Classics.

Forrest, Leon. 1994. *Relocations of the Spirit: Collected Essays*. Kisco, NY: Asphodel Press.

Foster, George Murphy "Pops" with Tom Stoddard. 1971. *The Autobiography of Pops Foster, New Orleans Jazzman*. Berkeley: University of California Press.

Garroutte, Eva Marie. 2003. *Real Indians: Identity and Survival of Native America*. Berkeley: University of California Press.

Gipson, Jennifer. 2016. "'A Strange, Ventriloquous Voice': Louisiana Creole, Whiteness, and the Racial Politics of Writing Orally." *The Journal of American Folklore* Vol. 129 (514): 459–485.

Glissant, Édouard. 1997. *Poetics of Relation*, translated by Betsy Wing. Ann Arbor: University of Michigan Press.

Graziano, Frank. 2004. *The Mystical Marriage of St. Rose of Lima*. Oxford: Oxford University Press.

Grenier, John. 2005. *The First Way of War: American War Making on the Frontier, 1607–1814*. Cambridge: Cambridge University Press.

Hahn, George. 2008. "King of Jazz." in *Louisiana Cultural Vistas* Fall: 56–61.

Hair, William Ivy. 1991. *The Kingfish and His Realm: The Life and Times of Huey P. Long*. Baton Rouge: Louisiana State University Press.

Hall, Gwendolyn Midlo. 1992. *Africans in Colonial Louisiana: The Development of Afro-Creole Culture in the Eighteenth Century*. Baton Rouge: Louisiana State University Press.

———. 1992. "The Formation of Afro-Creole Culture" in *Creole New Orleans: Race and Americanization*. Edited by Arnold R. Hirsch and Joseph Logsdon. Baton Rouge: Louisiana State University Press: 58–87.

Hanger, Kimberly S. 1997. *Bounded Lives, Bounded Places: Free Black Society in Colonial New Orleans, 1769–1803*. Durham: Duke University Press.

Hearn, Lafcadio. 1885. *Gombo Zhebes: Little Dictionary of Creole Proverbs*. Bedford, Massachusetts: Applewood Books.

Hersch, Charles B. 2007. *Subversive Sounds: Race and the Birth of Jazz in New Orleans*. Chicago: University of Chicago Press.

Hirsch, Arnold. 2007. "Fade to Black: Hurricane Katrina and The Disappearance of Creole New Orleans." *The Journal of American History* Vol. 94 (3): 752–761.

Ingersol, Thomas N. 1996. "The Slave Trade and the Ethnic Diversity of Louisiana's Slave Community." *Louisiana History: The Journal of the Louisiana Historical Association* Vol. 37 (2): 133–161.

Jackson, Michael. 1998. *Minima Ethnographica: Intersubjectivity and the Anthropological Project*. Chicago: University of Chicago Press.

Jacobs, Claude F. and Andrew J. Kaslow. 1991. *The Spiritual Churches of New Orleans: Origins, Beliefs, and Rituals of an African American Religion*. Knoxville: University of Tennessee Press.

Johnson, Jerah. 1992. "Colonial New Orleans: A Fragment of the Eighteenth-Century French Ethos" in *Creole New Orleans: Race and Americanization*. Edited by Arnold Hirsch and Joseph Logsdon. Baton Rouge: Louisiana State University Press: 12–57.

Jones, Gavin. 1999. *Strange Talk: The Politics of Dialect Literature in Gilded Age America*. Berkeley: University of California Press.

Jones, Gayl. 1991. *Liberating Voices: Oral Traditions in African American Literature*. Cambridge: Harvard University Press.

Jordan, Rosan Augusta and Frank De Caro. 1996. "'In This Folk-Lore Land': Race, Class, Identity, and Folklore Studies in Louisiana." *The Journal of American Folklore* Vol. 109 (431): 31–59.

Jolivétte, Andrew. 2007. *Louisiana Creoles: Cultural Recovery and Mixed-Race Native American Identity*. Lanham, MD: Lexington Books.

Jung, C.G. 1990 [1956]. *The Archetypes and the Collective Unconscious*. Translated by R.F.C. Hull. New York: Princeton University Press.

Long, Carolyn Morrow. 2006. *A New Orleans Voudou Priestess: The Legend and Reality of Marie Laveau*. Gainsville: University Press of Florida.

Keil, Charles. 1992. "Culture, Music, Collaborative Learning" in *The Politics of Culture and Creativity: Essays in Honor of Stanley Diamond, A Critique of Civilization, Vol. 2*. Edited by Christine Ward Gailey. Gainsville: University of Florida Press.

Kein, Sybil. 2000. "The Use of Louisiana Creole in Southern Literature" in *Creole: The History and Legacy of Louisiana's Free People of Color*. Edited by Sybil Kein. Baton Rouge: Louisiana State University Press: 117–155.

Kein, Sybil. 1981. *Gumbo People*. Edited by Ulysses Ricard, Jr. New Orleans: Margaret Media, Inc.

Kelley, Robin D.G. 2002. *Freedom Dreams: The Black Radical Imagination*. Boston: Beacon Press.

Klinger, Thomas A. 2003. *If I Could Turn My Tongue Like That: The Creole Language of Pointe Coupee Parish, Louisiana*. Baton Rouge: Louisiana State University Press.

Kniffen, Fred B., Hiram F. Gregory, and George A. Stokes. 1987. *The Historic Tribes of Louisiana: From 1542 to the Present*. Baton Rouge: Louisiana State University Press.

Kulka, Jon. 2004. *A Wilderness So Immense: The Louisiana Purchase and the Destiny of America*. New York: First Anchor Books.

Kunkel, Paul A. 1959. "Modifications in Louisiana Negro Legal Status Under Louisiana Constitutions, 1812–1957." *The Journal of Negro History* Vol. 44 (1): 1–25.

LaChance, Paul F. 1992. "The Foreign French" in *Creole New Orleans: Race and Americanization*. Edited by Arnold R. Hirsch and Joseph Logdson. Baton Rouge: Louisiana State University Press: 101–130.

Lagarde, Roland. 1989. "A Contemporary Pilgrimage: Personal Testimony of Blessed Katharine Drexel's Charism." *U.S. Catholic Historian* Vol. 8 (1/2): 47–50.

Lalonde, Michèle. 1968. "Speak White." *Dormir Jamais*: http://dormirjamais.org/speakwhite. Last accessed February 3, 2018.

Leglaunec, Jean-Pierre. 2005. "A Directory of Ships with Slave Cargoes, Louisiana, 1772-1808." *Louisiana History: The Journal of the Louisiana Historical Association* Vol. 46 (2): 211–230.

Leupin, Alexandre and Francis Pavy. 2018. *Francis Pavy: Visions*. Baton Rouge: Louisiana State Press.

Lief, Shane and Jeffrey Darensbourg. 2015. "Popular Music and Indigenous Languages in Louisiana." *The Music of Endangered Languages: Foundation of Endangered Languages XIX-NOLA 2015*. Proceedings of the 19th FEL Conference.

Lipsitz, George. 1998. "Mardi Gras Indians: Carnival and Counter-Narrative in Black New Orleans." *Cultural Critique* Vol. 10: 99–121.

Lomax, Alan. 2001 [1950]. *Mister Jelly Roll: The Fortunes of Jelly Roll Morton, New Orleans Creole and "Inventor of Jazz."* Berkeley: University of California Press.

Maddox, Camee. 2015. "Dance, Drum, and the Defense of Cultural Citizenship: Bèlè's Revival in Contemporary Martinique." Ph.D. Dissertation. University of Florida.

Mattern, Mark. 1997. "Let the Good Times Unroll: Music and Race Relations in Southwest Louisiana." *Black Music Research Journal* Vol. 17 (2): 159–168.

Medley, Keith Weldon. 2014. *Black Life in Old New Orleans*. Gretna, Louisiana: Pelican Publishing Company.

McCreum, Robert, William Cran, and Robert MacNeil. 1986. *The Story of English*. New York: Elisabeth Sifton Books/Viking.

McCusker, John. 2012. *Creole Trombone: Kid Ory and the Early Years of Jazz*. Jackson: University Press of Mississippi.

McWhorter, John. 2017. *Talking Back, Talking Black: Truths About America's Lingua Franca*. New York: Bellevue Literary Press.

———. 2009. *Our Magnificent Bastard Tongue: The Untold Story of English*. New York: Avery.

Murphy, Joseph M. 2015. *Botánicas: Sacred Spaces of Healing and Devotion in Urban America*. Jackson: University Press of Mississippi.

Nathan and the Zydeco Cha Chas. 1998. *Follow Me Chicken*. Cambridge, MA: Rounder Records.

Natsis, James J. 1999. "Legislation and Language: The Politics of Speaking French in Louisiana." *The French Review* Vol. 73 (2): 325–331.

Needham, Maureen. 2002. "The War of the Quadrilles: Creoles vs. Americans (1804)" in *I See America Dancing: Selected Readings, 1685-2000*. Edited by Maureen Needham. Urbana: University of Illinois Press: 66–72.

Oldenburg, Ray. 2001. *Celebrating the Third Place: Inspiring Stories About the "Great Good Places" in the Heart of Our Communities*. New York: Marlowe and Company.

Olivier, Rick (photography) and Ben Sandmel (text). 1999. *Zydeco!* Jackson: The University Press of Mississippi.

O'Malley, George E. 2009. "Beyond the Middle Passage: Slave Migration from the Caribbean to North America, 1619–1807." *William and Mary Quarterly* Vol. LXVI (1): 125–172.

Orso, Ethelyn. 1990. *The St. Joseph Altar Traditions of South Louisiana*. Lafayette: The Center for Louisiana Studies, University of Southwestern Louisiana.

Osbey, Brenda Marie. 1997. *All Saints: New and Selected Poems*. Baton Rouge: Louisiana State University Press: 108–114.

Picone, Michael C. 1997. "Enclave Dialect Contraction: An

External Overview of Louisiana French" in *American Speech* Vol. 72 (2): 117–153.

Post, Lauren C. 1962. "Some Notes on the Attakapas Indians of Southwest Louisiana." *Journal of Louisiana History* 3: 221–243.

Prud'homme-Cranford, Rain. 2019. "Summoning Swamp Songs: Decolonizing Creole-Indigenous Textural Tributaries" in *Swamp Souths: Literary and Cultural Ecologies*. Edited by Eric G Anderson and Kirstin Squint. Baton Rouge: Louisiana State University Press.

—— and Carolyn M. Dunn. 2017. "Grandma's Zydeco Stomp Dance." *World Literature Today*. May: https://www.worldliteraturetoday.org/2017/may/grandmas-zydeco-stomp-dance-patchwork-poem-rain-prudhomme-cranford-carolyn-m-dunn. Last accessed September 29, 2018.

Reckdahl, Katy. 2004. "Down on the Corner" in *The Gambit* May 18: https://www.theadvocate.com/gambit/new_orleans/news/article_b0d9984c-5201-5e82-a961-1dbb038b7eed.html. Last accessed February 5, 2019.

Reilly, Timothy F. 2002. "The Louisiana Colonization Society and the Protestant Missionary, 1830–1860." *Louisiana History: The Journal of the Louisiana Historical Association* Vol. 43 (4): 433–477.

Roach, Joseph. 1992. "Mardi Gras Indians and Others: Genealogies of American Performance." *Theatre Journal* 44 (4): 461–483.

Rogers, Bethany. 2008. "The Maple Leaf Bar" in *Cornerstones: Celebrating the Everyday Monuments and Gathering Places of New Orleans Neighborhoods*. Edited by Rachel Breunlin. New Orleans: The Neighborhood Story Project at the University of New Orleans Press.

Rose, Deborah Bird. 2004. *Reports from A Wild Country: Ethics for Decolonisation*. Sydney, Australia: University of New South Wales Press.

Rosenthal, Judy. 1998. *Possession, Ecstasy, and Law in Ewe Voodoo*. Charlottesville: University of Virginia Press.

Rush, Dana. 2013. *Vodun in Coastal Benin: Unfinished, Open-ended, Global*. Nashville: Vanderbilt University Press.

Russell, Sarah. 1999. "Ethnicity, Commerce, and Community on Lower Louisiana's Plantation Frontier, 1803-1828." *Louisiana History: The Journal of the Louisiana Historical Association* Vol. 40 (4): 389–405.

Saloy, Mona Lisa. 2005. *Red Beans and Ricely Yours*. Kirksville, Missouri: Truman State University Press.

Sheringham, Olivia. 2012. "From Creolization to Relation: An Interview with Patrick Chamoiseu" in *Oxford Diasporas Programme*: https://www.imi-n.org/files/news/patrickchamoiseauinterview_f.pdf. Last accessed February 2, 2019.

Sidrack, Ben. 1971. *Black Talk*. New York: Holt, Rinehart, and Winston.

Sluyter, Andrew. 2012. "The Role of Blacks in Establishing Cattle Ranching in Louisiana in the Eighteenth Century." *Agricultural History* Vol. 86 (2): 41–67.

Smith, Michael P. 1994. *Mardi Gras Indians*. Gretna: Pelican Publishing Company.

Snedeker, Rebecca. 2013. "Holding It Together, Falling Apart" in *Unfathomable City: A New Orleans Atlas*. Edited by Rebecca Solnit and Rebecca Snedeker. Berkeley: University of California Press.

Spitzer, Nick. 2003. "Monde Crèole: The Cultural World of French Louisiana Creoles and the Creolization of World Cultures." *The Journal of American Folklore* Vol. 116 (459): 57–72.

———. 1986. "Zydeco and Mardi Gras: Black Creole Ethnohistory, Ethnography, and Expressive Culture in Rural French Louisiana." *A Report to the Jean Lafitte National Historical Park*.

Starr, S. Frederick, ed. 2001. *Inventing New Orleans: Writings of Lafcadio Hearn*. Jackson: University Press of Mississippi.

Students at the Center. 2003. *The Long Ride: A Collection of Student Writings Based on the Events that are Part of the Long Struggle for Civil Rights and Social Justice in New Orleans*. New Orleans: Students at the Center, a Program of the Renaissance Project.

Sublette, Ned. 2009. *The World That Made New Orleans: From Spanish Silver to Congo Square*. Chicago: Lawrence Hill Books.

Sunpie and the Louisiana Sunspots. 2013. *Island Man*. New Orleans. BFR Records.

Szwed, John. 2010. *Alan Lomax: The Man Who Recorded the World*. New York: Viking.

Takaki, Ronald. 1993. *A Different Mirror: A History of Multicultural America*. Boston: Back Bay Books/Little, Brown & Company.

Tallant, Robert. 1984 [1946]. *Voodoo in New Orleans*. Gretna, LA: Pelican Publishing Company.

Taussig, Michael. 1993. *Mimesis and Alterity: A Particular History of the Senses*. New York: Routledge.

The Picayune's Guide to New Orleans. 1896. New Orleans: Nicholson & Company.

Thompson, Robert Farris. 1993. *Face of the Gods: Art and Altars of Africa and African Americans*. New York: Prestell for the Museum of African Art.

Thompson, Shirley. 2001. "'Ah, Toucoutou, ye conin vous': History and Memory in Creole New Orleans." *American Quarterly* Vol. 53 (2): 232–266.

Thiong'o, Ngugi Wa. 1997. *Decolonising the Mind: The Politics of Language in African Literature*. London/Portsmouth, New Hampshire: James Currey/Heinemann.

Tinker, Edward Larocque. 1953. *Creole City: Its Past and Its People*. London: Longmans Green Company.

Tisserand, Michael. 1998. *The Kingdom of Zydeco*. New York: Arcade Publishing

Tregle, Joseph G. 1992. "Creoles and Americans" in *Creole New Orleans: Race and Americanization*. Edited by Arnold R. Hirsch and Joseph Logsdon. Baton Rouge: Louisiana State University Press: 131–185.

Trépanier, Cécyle. 1991. "The Cajunization of French Louisiana: Forging a Regional Identity." *The Geographical Journal* Vol. 157 (2): 161–171.

Usner, Daniel H. 2018. *American Indians in Early New Orleans: From Calumet to Raquette*. Baton Rouge: Louisiana State University Press.

———. 1998. *American Indians in the Lower Mississippi Valley*. Lincoln: University of Nebraska Press.

Valdman, Albert. 1998. *Ann pale kreyòl: An Introductory Course in Haitian Creole*. Bloomington: Creole Institute, Indiana University.

Valdman, Albert, Thomas A. Klinger, Margaret M. Marshall, and Kevin J. Rottet. 1998. *Dictionary of Louisiana Creole*. Bloomington: Indiana University Press.

van den Berk, Tjeu. 2012. *Jung on Art: The Autonomy of the Creative Drive*. New York: Psychology Press.

Verdin, Monique. 2013. "Southward into the Vanishing Lands" in *Unfathomable City: A New Orleans Atlas*. Edited by Rebecca Solnit and Rebecca Snedeker. Berkeley: University of California Press.

Voisin, Erin. 2008. "San Maló Remembered" Masters Thesis. Department of Anthropology and Geography, Louisiana State University.

von Franz, Marie-Louise. 1980. *Alchemy: An Introduction to the Symbolism and the Psychology*. Toronto: Inner City Books.

Waddell, E. 1979. "French Louisiana: an outpost of 'l'Amerique francaise' or another country and another culture?" in *Québec: Projet Louisiane, Document de travail No. 4* Départment de Géographie, Université Laval. Published in French in Cah. Géog. Du Québ. 23 (59): 199–216.

Wagner, Jacob. 2004. "The Myth of Liberty Place: Race and Public Memory in New Orleans, 1874–1993." Ph.D. Dissertation. University of New Orleans.

Walcott, Derek. 1998. *What the Twilight Says*. New York: Farrar, Straus, and Giroux.

Ward, Martha. 2004. *Voodoo Queen: The Spirited Lives of Marie Laveau*. Jackson: University Press of Mississippi.

Welburn, Ron. 2002. "A Most Secret Identity: Native American Assimilation and Identity Resistance in African America" in *Confounding the Color Line: The Indian-Black Experience in North America*. Edited by James F. Brooks. Lincoln: University of Nebraska Press: 292–320.

Wehmeyer, Stephen. 2012. "Playing Dead: The Northside Skull and Bone Gang" in *In Extremis: Life and Death in 21st Century Haitian Ar*t. Edited by Donald Cosentino. Los Angeles: UCLA's Fowler Museum for Cultural History..

———. 2000. "Indian Altars of the Spiritual Church: Kongo Echoes in New Orleans." *African Arts* Vol. 33 (4): 62–69+95–96.

Willey, Nathan. 1866. "Education of the Colored Population of Louisiana" in *Harper's New Monthly Magazine* July: 248.

Winer, Lise, ed. 2008. *Dictionary of English/Creole of Trinidad and Tobago, on Historical Principles*. Québec: McGill-Queen's University Press.

Wylie, Arlet and Sam Wylie. 2005. *Between Piety and Desire*. Edited by Rachel Breunlin. New Orleans: Neighborhood Story Project at the University of New Orleans Press.

Zinn, Howard. 1980. *A People's History of the United States*. New York: Harper Perennial.